NORWICH

ARCHAEOLOGY OF A FINE CITY

NORWICH

ARCHAEOLOGY OF A FINE CITY

BRIAN AYERS

AMBERLEY

First published 2009

Amberley Publishing Plc
Cirencester Road, Chalford,
Stroud, Gloucestershire, GL6 8PE

www.amberley-books.com

British Library Cataloguing in Publication Data.
A catalogue record for this book is available from the British Library.

ISBN 978 1 84868 372 3

Typesetting and Origination by Diagraf (www.diagraf.net)
Printed in Great Britain

CONTENTS

For my Mother and Father
Sheila and Vin Ayers

PREFACE

In 1698 Celia Fiennes, the celebrated traveller and journal writer, visited Norwich. She climbed the castle hill to see the whole city from its vantage point and was impressed with the view. 'Its a vast place and takes up a large tract of ground its 6 miles in compass ... the whole Citty lookes like what it is, a rich thriveing industrious place'. Later, when she walked about the streets, she was shown 'a wall made of flints that are headed very finely and cut so exactly square and even, to shutt in one to another, that the whole wall is made without cement at all they say, but it appears to be very little if any mortar, it looks well very smooth shineing and black'.

These two observations, the general and the particular, but both concerned largely with the physical aspect of Norwich, illustrated the approach which I tried to take in this book when it first appeared in 1994. It was a summary of the archaeology of the city, attempting to assess the development of Norwich in terms of the details of its material culture. This revision does not depart from this established format but, as before, it of necessity also requires a general historical framework upon which to hang itself. Such a framework is provided by the chronological approach of the book and reference to inescapable events such as the Norman Conquest. Nevertheless, in order that the text be not too inhibited by this need to explain the historical context, a summary table of events is also provided.

Norwich, a regional capital of great importance in the Middle Ages, is still one of the foremost centres of East Anglia. The main theme of this book is an assessment of how the city grew physically, socially and economically over the past millennium, studying how archaeology is helping to clarify these processes, with emphasis being placed upon the history of the city as a community peopled by citizens who had needs of food, shelter, security and spiritual nourishment.

In this way I hope that the book will be of more than local interest, for the archaeology of Norwich embodies much which is common to the experience of communities elsewhere. Norwich was an important city in the national and international economy; study of its archaeology helps to shed light on developments across much of north-western Europe. It is not, however, the intention that this book should seek continually to highlight such connections;

1 Twelfth-century stone building excavated at St Martin-at-Palace Plain (Brian Ayers)

it is foremost a summary of archaeological discovery in Norwich, not a critique of such discoveries in the context of urban development in England or northern Europe as a whole.

The archaeology of Norwich is taken to mean an all-embracing discipline, one which examines material evidence but puts it into a context provided by other forms of historical research, such as the study of topography, cartography, documents, place-names and numismatics. The book explores, therefore, how archaeological observation informs and supplements existing models of urban history.

Norwich is, to some extent, a city of superlatives. The largest walled town of any urban centre in England during the Middle Ages (larger than London and Southwark combined), it contains more surviving medieval churches than any town in northern Europe and was the richest provincial city of the country for much of the seventeenth and eighteenth centuries, with the crowning appellation of 'Second City'. This exceptionally large city has a correspondingly diverse historic environment. It is blessed with a wealth of historic buildings, an exceptional collection of medieval documentation, a long and honourable antiquarian tradition, nationally important museums and an extraordinarily wide-ranging tradition of historical and archaeological enquiry. It would be pleasing to present this book as a synthesis of all this; regrettably that cannot be the case.

I have instead tried to give an overview of the growth of the city as seen by one who is interested in both the processes of urban development and the effects of that development. I have sought to draw on a wide variety of sources and disciplines in order to convey an impression of both the city at various periods and the different ways in which information is being gleaned.

Inevitably some aspects of both the city and the sources get short shrift. I am conscious that much more could have been written on the surviving churches or on the importance of the textile industry to the city, to cite but two examples. To have done so, however, would have created an imbalance in the book which is essentially a summary overview of the medieval and post-medieval city. It is also largely a view confined to the historic walled core of Norwich although the greater city and its hinterland are necessarily important to a contextual understanding of that view.

It would not have been possible to write this book at all but for the great help which I have received from friends and colleagues, the numbers of whom have increased since the first edition of this book. As before, many of the ideas expressed here owe much to conversations with the late Alan Carter (formerly director of the Norwich Survey) and with Barbara Green (formerly keeper of archaeology at Norwich Castle Museum). Both of them have contributed enormously to a better understanding of the growth of the city and my debt to each remains very considerable.

I continue to owe much to other colleagues, particularly to Malcolm Atkin, Bill Milligan, Robert Smith and Margot Tillyard for providing me with formative insights into the archaeology, buildings and documentary history of Norwich. I also continue to benefit from the generosity of others who give me new information, discuss problems with me and, most importantly, point out when I am wrong! The list was long in 1994 and is still growing. Thanks then went to Nick Arber, Chris Barringer, David Cubitt, the late Keith Darby, Alan Davison, Alayne Fenner, Eric Fernie, Roberta Gilchrist, Stephen Heywood, Sandy Heslop, Sarah Jennings, Derek Manning, Mary Manning, the late Sue Margeson, Peter Murphy, Vic Nierop-Reading, Andrew Rogerson, Elizabeth Rutledge and Norman Smith. They must now also go to Penny Dunn and Carole Rawcliffe. Ideas of many of these people appear in this book.

I receive great help from my colleagues in the Norfolk Archaeology & Environment division who give me much new information and many new ideas.

I remain especially indebted to my long-time colleague Jayne Bown, but thanks in 1994 also went to Niall Donald, Phil Emery, Julia Huddle, Irena Lentowicz, Kenneth Penn, Jez Reeve, Andy Shelley, Liz Shepherd and Heather Wallis. These thanks need to be made again with additional gratitude to Andy Hutcheson and John Percival. I am particularly grateful to both Andys, Liz, Heather and John for providing me with information on work on King Street, at the Millennium Library site, at the castle and at the cathedral.

In 1994 I received much helpful criticism from colleagues who read either the complete text in draft or parts of it. My greatest debt was to Barbara Green who read the entire original text, made many useful comments and saved me from one or two howlers. Trevor Ashwin kindly read the prehistoric section, also saved me from howlers, and gave me useful new information. Robert Smith read and discussed with me the chapters which include details concerning the buildings of the city; again I was saved from myself. Chris Barringer read the final chapter and gently highlighted the odd startling omission. Jayne Bown, Niall Donald, Jez Reeve, Andy Shelley and Liz Shepherd also all generously provided me with useful comments on the text. Parts of the revised text have been read by both Andy Shelley and Liz Shepherd and who, once again, have assisted me by pointing out errors or misunderstandings.

The entire 1994 draft was read by Alan Browne as a non-archaeologist, giving me useful and trenchant comment as well as ideas for the glossary. Neither he nor any of the above individuals, of course, is responsible for any of the errors which no doubt remain.

Many of the illustrations of this book have been provided from the archives of the Norfolk Archaeological Unit with the air photographs from those of the Norfolk Landscape Archaeology Section, both organisations being part of the Archaeology & Environment division of the Norfolk Museums & Archaeology Service. Individual N.A.U. photographers and illustrators are credited in the captions as are all other individuals and organisations who have kindly permitted illustrations to be used. Special thanks are owed to Norma Watt of the Art Department at Norwich Castle Museum for all her assistance concerning early paintings and drawings of the city. I am also most grateful to David Wicks for his assistance in providing photographs.

In 1994 I was particularly in the debt of my brother David who gave me a computer which enabled me to word-process the text. For this revision, I must thank my wife Robina McNeil who has most generously re-typed those parts of the disk which had become corrupt and unreadable, thus enabling me to work more quickly on the text. She too has provided me with critical comment and, most importantly, encouraged me to produce the work. In this she gallantly took on the burden previously shouldered by Lynn, Emily and Megan. I owe Robina a great deal and my greatest thanks, and love, go to her.

PREFACE TO 2009 EDITION

This third edition of the book contains further revision, taking account of recent work in the city. Large-scale excavations have been less in number in recent years although interventions on both Palace Street and Fishergate were sizable projects by modern standards. Significant publications have also emerged in the last five years (notably a two-volume multi-authored history of Norwich) and these are mentioned in an updated section on Further Reading. I remain indebted to the colleagues mentioned above but also to the following: David Adams, for not only generously sharing information with me but frequently providing me with very thoughtful insights into the development of the city; Barbara Crawford, who has the marvellous ability to take my accepted ideas and rework them to produce convincing new concepts; and Chris King whose work on the elite houses of Norwich opened my eyes to the potential of these buildings for increasing understanding of the society of late medieval and post-medieval Norwich.

As noted above, work on the second edition was assisted greatly by my late wife Robina McNeil who died in 2007. A revised work cannot be a memorial to her but she was my finest helpmate, my best critic and my great love. She was an archaeologist with a deep affection for towns and she would have been pleased to see this volume reissued.

1

THE ORIGINS AND
EARLY GROWTH OF SETTLEMENT

Any assessment of the archaeology of Norwich must start with its geography. The physical topography of the city itself has always been affected by this geography while the location of Norwich has influenced not only its economy but also the self-view of its citizens This self-view is evident from early maps of the city. These nearly always emphasise its location within a surrounding agricultural area. Fat sheep can be seen within and without the walls on Cuningham's plan of 1558, while cornfields and windmills are testimony to the abundance of the hinterland. The implied geographical importance of Norwich even allowing for local propaganda is clear.

The city stands astride the Wensum, a meandering East Anglian river which is still, although barely, tidal within the built up area. The river enters the historic core from the north-west, its relatively wide valley becoming constricted as the stream turns eastwards to pass north of the land now dominated by the castle and cathedral. This constriction is caused by two areas of relatively high ground, that of Mousehold Heath to the north and east, and that of the Ber Street escarpment to the south and west. East of the cathedral, the river turns south once more and gradually the valley opens out again until it merges with that of the river Yare, into which the Wensum flows south-east of the ancient (and modern) city.

The constriction of the river valley led to the accumulation of glacial deposits, notably sands and gravels, in the valley bottom on the margins of the river. The underlying geology is chalk, with generous inclusions of flint, and is surmounted in places by Norwich crag (a Pleistocene deposit of a shelly sandstone). The sands and gravels can be up to seven metres (23ft) thick and form well-drained terraces, ideal for early settlement and for affording access to, and crossing of, the river.

The river was fed by tributary streams, known locally as 'cockeys', which flowed into it from either bank. The largest of these, the 'Great Cockey', occupied its own small valley to the west of the Ber Street escarpment. It rose near present-day All Saint's Green and flowed via Red Lion Street, White Lion Street, Little London Street and School Lane, northward to the river. It was culverted by the eighteenth century, but its outflow can still be seen near St George's Bridge, and damage to the culvert by modern development can lead to flooding, as occurred on Castle Street in 1962.

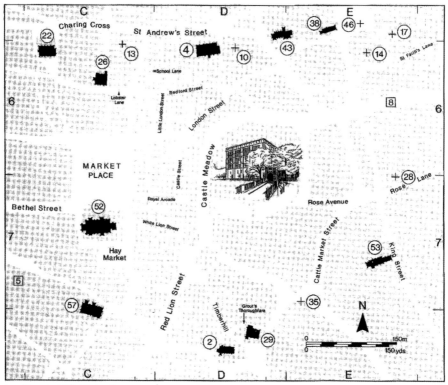

Above is detail of central area opposite.

Key to Churches and Religious Houses
Churches are represented by a circle, Religious Houses by a square.

○ CHURCHES

1	All Saints Fyebriggate	19	St George Colegate	40	St Mary Coslany
2	All Saints Westlegate	20	St George Tombland	41	St Mary-in-the-Marsh
3	Christ Church	21	St Giles	42	St Mathew
	Holy Trinity	22	St Gregory	43	St Michael at Pleas
4	St Andrew	23	St Helen	44	St Michael Conesford
5	St Augustine	24	St James	45	St Michael Coslany
6	St Bartholomew	25	St John de Sepulchre	46	St Michael Tombland
7	St Benedict	26	St John Maddermarket	47	St Michael-at-Thorn
8	St Botolph	27	St John the Baptist	48	St Olaf Conesford
9	St Catherine	28	St John the Evangelist	49	St Olave Pitt Street
10	St Christopher	29	St John Timberhill	50	St Paul
11	St Clement Colegate	30	St Julian	51	St Peter Hungate
12	St Clement Conesford	31	St Laurence	52	St Peter Mancroft
13	St Crouche	32	St Margaret in combusto	53	St Peter Parmentergate
14	St Cuthbert	33	St Margaret Newbridge	54	St Peter Southgate
15	St Edmund	34	St Margaret Westwick	55	St Saviour
16	St Edward	35	St Martin in Balliva	56	SS Simon and Jude
17	St Ethelbert	36	St Martin-at-Oak	57	St Stephen
18	St Etheldreda	37	St Martin-at-Palace	58	St Swithin
		38	St Mary the Less	59	St Vedast
		39	St Mary Combuste	60	St Anne

□ RELIGIOUS HOUSES

1	Augustinian Friary
2	Carmelite Friary
3	Carrow Priory
4	Cathedral Priory
5	College of St Mary in the Fields
6	Dominican Friary (first site)
7	Dominican Friary (second site)
8	Franciscan Friary
9	Great Hospital
10	Hildebrond's Hospital
11	Lazar House
12	Norman Hospital
13	St Leonard's Priory
14	St Michael's Chapel
15	St William's Chapel

2a and *2b* Plan of Norwich within the walls (Karen Guffogg)

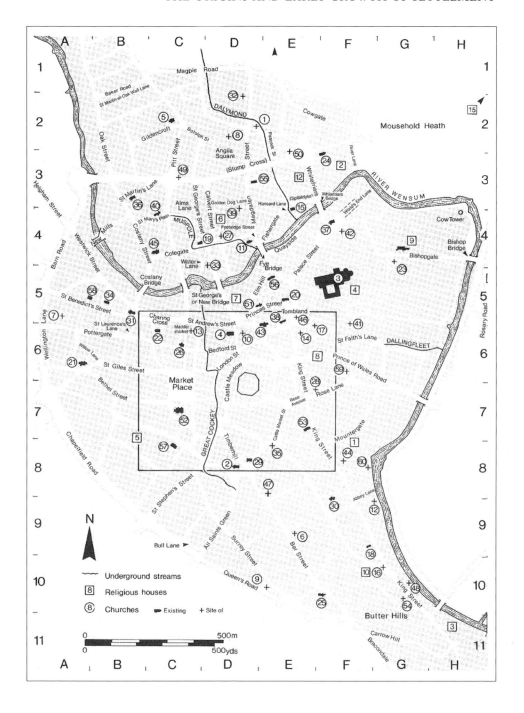

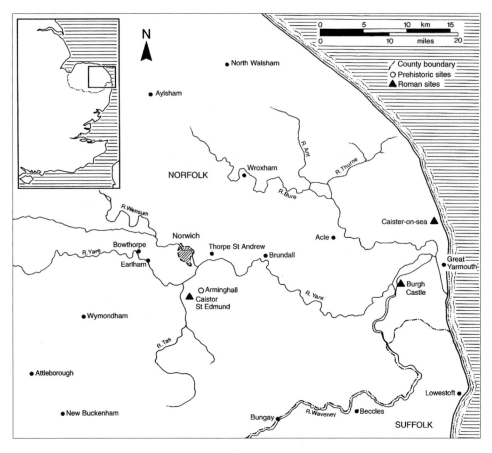

3 Map of Norwich in its region (Karen Guffogg)

Other streams flowed into the river from both the north and south banks. The largest on the north side was the Dalymond which rose in Old Catton, entered the area of the walled city at Magpie Road, formed a parish boundary as far as Magdalen Street, then flowed down at least part of Rattenrowe to enter the river at Water (now Hansard) Lane. This stream was observed still running during a watching brief off Rattenrowe in 1985.

The location of these streams clearly had an effect upon early settlement. They provided water for domestic and industrial purposes but they also defined areas of the developing community. It will be seen that the alignment of certain streets and boundaries is due to the presence of such tributaries. An important aspect of archaeological work continues to be the attempt to reconstruct the alignments and nature of these geographical features and their small valleys, the masking of which in recent centuries has obscured the early topography of the city. The steep hills to the south and north-east, together with the cockey valleys, present a landscape which belies the popular notion of Norfolk as 'very flat'. Norwich is

4 Excavations at Carrow Road football stadium (NAU Archaeology)

indeed one of the more hilly cities of lowland England and current investigation is beginning to indicate that it was originally more hilly still. Work in both the valley of the Great Cockey and near the outflow of the Muspole (on the north bank) has shown that infilling has flattened out the natural topography while recent excavation south of the river behind Quayside suggests a previously unsuspected small tributary valley now infilled.

The hill-slopes and gravel terraces on either bank of the river, while good for settlement, are not necessarily ideal areas for the archaeologist. Most of Norwich is well-drained, with moisture running off through the gravels and chalk. This inhibits the development of waterlogged anaerobic deposits and the preservation of organic material on archaeological sites in the city is generally poor. Such deposits usually only exist at the river margins.

The building stone of the city is also poor. There are no local supplies of good quality freestone or, indeed, of any freestone. In consequence most buildings were constructed for many centuries in timber or flint, with a chalk and flint rubble wall core. Freestone dressings were expensive and thus tended to be robbed from disused buildings. Archaeological interpretation can be impeded when an excavated wall footing consists solely of flint rubble with its distinctive dressings missing. Archaeological evidence is therefore often hard won, the more so in that much of the city has been occupied intensively for a millennium. Conversely, however, the existence of slopes and the resulting attempts to level or reduce these can often lead to situations where deposits and features are remarkably well-preserved due to deliberate burial.

Norwich, like other important East Anglian towns such as Ipswich and Thetford, is not Roman in origin but grew to prominence in the Anglo-Saxon and Anglo-Scandinavian periods. The settlement's name does not appear in any known document before the 980s; the earliest map is a sketch of about 1540 and the earliest illustrations of topographical use also date from the sixteenth century. It follows that the evidence of the urban topography and archaeology, supported by allied disciplines such as place-name study and numismatics, provide the only keys to an understanding of origins and early growth.

PRE-URBAN SETTLEMENT

It will become clear that those settlements which were eventually to form the nucleus of the modern city appear to date from the mid to late seventeenth century. The area of medieval and modern Norwich, however, masks an environment which has been settled in one form or another since prehistoric times. The archaeology of the pre-urban environment is as much part of the history of Norwich as the development of the city itself.

Palaeolithic (*c.*500,000-10,000 BC) and Mesolithic (*c.*10,000-4500 BC) material is naturally sparce. Palaeolithic flints, including a handaxe, were reported from Mousehold Heath in 1933 and 1974, whilst handaxes and flakes were recovered at Carrow, immediately south of the medieval city wall in 1927-8 and 1963. Large numbers of Palaeolithic flints were recovered from gravel pits in Whitlingham Marsh in the 1920s while flakes now thought to be Mesolithic were reported from Carrow (in 1887), from the top of Carrow Hill (before 1947) and at Boundary Road (in 1964). The most startling evidence, however, was recovered in 2002 during excavations in advance of a new south stand at Carrow Road football ground. Upper Palaeolithic flint debitage was located on a sandy island beneath peat around which the river braided, material clearly brought from elsewhere to the island and worked *in situ*, presumably for hunting.

The peat was examined slightly further upstream during development of the Riverside site in 1998. Here an extensive palaeochannel of the river Wensum

5 Arminghall Henge from the air (Derek A. Edwards; © Norfolk Museums & Archaeology Service)

provided evidence of Mesolithic activity. While this and the other discoveries were not located in the historic centre of the medieval city, excavations in 1985 on Fishergate, next to Wensum, also uncovered a thick peat deposit above the river gravels. Environmental evidence, together with radiocarbon dating, of the lower levels of this peat indicated that the Mesolithic valley in about 7000 BC was wooded and suitable for human occupation. It is reasonable to suppose that the extensive low-lying marshy areas of the river valley were exploited for fish and fowl in the Upper Palaeolithic and Mesolithic periods, the later material perhaps associated with settlement on the river margins (as evidenced by a blade of possible Mesolithic date found at the corner of Cowgate and Magdalen Street in 1974).

Early Neolithic finds (c.4500-2500 BC) in the greater Norwich area are almost as sparce as those of Palaeolithic and Mesolithic date, but later Neolithic (c.2500-2000 BC) and Bronze Age (c.2000-800 BC) activity is becoming increasingly notable in the archaeological record. Stray finds are recorded from a number of city-centre sites, such as King Street (before 1898), at the site of the City Hall (in 1935) and dredged from the river Wensum (in 1950). Most recently, work at the Busseys Garage site, between Quayside and Palace Street, in 2000, not only produced flints of Late Neolithic or Early Bronze Age date but also post-holes of a building associated with fragments of a Biconical Urn dating to the mid second millennium BC.

This rare survival of structural evidence has been paralleled by work in 1999 at The Oaks in Harvey Lane, Thorpe, where elements of a rectangular structure at least 5.70m by 2.50m were recorded. Such discoveries in the area of Greater Norwich form the bulk of Neolithic and Bronze Age evidence. The Oaks lies to the north of the river Yare at the top of a substantial slope but most discoveries have been made in the river valleys and on hills to the south of the city. Recent river valley examples include a small post-hole structure from Bowthorpe together with a large pit or depression with quantities of Beaker pottery, both discovered in 2000. More extensive work took place on the edge of the valley in Eaton in 1971 when excavation of an area exceeding 6500 square metres uncovered a site of Neolithic settlement.

A nationally important Neolithic monument survives south of Norwich as a buried archaeological feature, again close to the river. This is the Arminghall Henge, a monument similar to the more famous henges of Wessex, but constructed of wood. It lies in the Yare valley a short distance above its confluence with the Wensum and was apparently a ceremonial monument, being first observed from the air in the 1920s and partially excavated in the 1930s. Henges are often found at river confluences in eastern England.

The Arminghall Henge is, however, merely the most important prehistoric monument in one of the most archaeologically rich areas of Norfolk. It is

6 *Venta Icenorum* Roman town, Caistor St Edmund (Crown Copyright/MOD)

surrounded by sites of late prehistoric, Romano-British and medieval date. Some survive as field monuments; others are known from antiquarian observations (as when Markshall cemetery was largely destroyed for a railway cutting); many have been plotted by field survey, many others by aerial photography.

The predominant archaeological feature is the ring-ditch or ploughed-out barrow, and aerial photography has now identified a considerable number of these. Some have been excavated, the most comprehensive series of excavations being those which preceded construction of the Norwich Southern Bypass (1989-90). Early Bronze Age ring-ditches were sampled at Bixley while five flattened barrows, including two of elaborate 'disc' type, were excavated at Harford Farm (*colour plate 2*). Earlier excavation had sampled barrows on Eaton Heath in the 1820s, a complex ring-ditch at Bowthorpe west of the city was excavated in 1979 (where a central burial was augmented by ten supplementary burials) and a ring-ditch at Sweet Briar Road north-west of the city was uncovered in 1982. Not all barrows have been destroyed; two survive at Ketteringham, not far from the edge of the modern city.

Although these Bronze Age monuments were all located in areas away from the historic core of Norwich, sufficient if patchy data survives within the centre to suggest similar activity here. It is possible that a fragmentary ditch uncovered at Bethel Street in 1999 may have been associated with a Bronze Age monument; the Bussey Garage discoveries have already been mentioned, the fragmentary remains of a barrow were uncovered on a prominent hilltop site at Ber Street in 2006, and occasional finds of archaeological material also hint at Bronze Age activity (such as the discovery of a barbed-and-tanged arrowhead in 1979 on the site of the Anglia Television offices). Bronze Age metalwork, however, is known from the area south and west of the city with finds reported from Unthank Road, Peckover Road and Eaton.

Evidence for Iron Age activity remains scarce within the Greater Norwich area although a Late Iron Age field system was uncovered in the 1971 work at Eaton. The major excavations at Harford Farm on the line of the Southern Bypass in 1990 uncovered at least six square-ditched enclosures which may date from the Iron Age. Five silver Icenian coins were found before 1940 in the vicinity of Weston Road and Iron Age material is also known from the village of Trowse, just south of the medieval city.

Roman finds from Norwich are much more common. This is not, however, as a result of intensive Roman occupation, but largely through the reuse of Roman material in later centuries, much of it probably pillaged from the important Roman settlement of *Venta Icenorium* or Caistor St Edmund some 5km (3 miles) south of the city. This much may be commemorated by the ancient doggerel couplet:

Caistor was a city when Norwich was none
Norwich was built with Caistor's stone

Caistor Roman town stands in the valley of the Tas, a tributary of the Yare, and dates from the first century with walls being added in the third. The site is now an open field (with a church in the south-east corner). The forum area and two *insulae* were excavated in the 1930s as was the south gate where a substantial masonry structure was located.

The hinterland of Caistor is also rich in Roman sites, notably that of a temple to the north-east, and the settlement was naturally served by roads, one of which probably ran northwards to cross the river Yare close to the present Lakenham Bridge before climbing Long John Hill to the Ber Street ridge which seperates the Yare and Wensum valleys. Here the road lay within the area of the later medieval core of Norwich and seems to have continued northward, probably bridging or fording the Great Cockey in the vicinity of Orford Hill, to a crossing of the Wensum at the southern end of Oak Street. It followed Oak Street to the line of the present-day Aylsham Road. An alternative alignment has been suggested along the river Wensum, following present-day King Street.

A north-to-south Roman road on either alignment would have been crossed by an east-to-west road (which has been given the name Holmestreet Way).

This second road ran from a probable Roman port at Brundall, situated on the river Yare to the east of Norwich, entered the area of the modern city at Pilling Park, crossed the river Wensum by means of a ford at Bishop Bridge, proceeded westward along a causeway which is now Bishopgate, passed through the site of the later cathedral (probably on the line of the nave), and ran westward along St Benedict's Street before leaving the area of the city via the Dereham Road. The Bishopgate causeway would have been necessary to keep the road out of the marsh and its existence seems to have been confirmed recently by structural problems in a Bishopgate house whose footings apparently straddle the causeway edge. Further east, this road too would have needed to cross the Great Cockey, somewhere near the foot of modern Exchange Street.

The probable alignment of these Roman roads indicates that the geographical importance of Norwich was recognized in the Roman period, even if not exploited by settlement. The crossing point on the Wensum of Holmestreet Way is the lowest ford on the river and, once bridged (probably in the thirteenth century), remained the lowest bridging point on the Wensum and Yare until the construction of the Haven Bridge at Great Yarmouth in the sixteenth century. It is possible, however, that there was a further crossing downstream of the modern city in the Roman period. Commercial excavations in 1961, some 30m (100ft) downstream of the confluence of the Wensum and Yare located a timber platform some 3.8m (12ft) below the level of the modern marsh, which may have formed a wharf or bridgehead.

Roman finds within Norwich do not indicate a settlement of any density, although pottery finds in 1974 and 1987 on sites adjacent to Magdalen Street suggest the possibility of a farmstead north of the river. Evidence for probable Romano-British field systems was also located south of the Wensum at the Chapelfield site in 2003. A barrow, which once lay on meadows where Thorpe Railway Station now stands, may also have been Romano-British in date. It was opened about 1826 by Woodward, who thought it 'Danish', and contained 'urns of rude workmanship' as well as cremated bone.

This presumed Roman barrow, immediately east of the medieval city, was supplemented by further discoveries some 2km (1¼ miles) further east in 1950. Construction of a tennis court at Stanley Avenue revealed two cremation burials of first-century date with rich grave goods. The first contained a handled flagon, a platter with cremated bones, a white bronze mirror with a wooden case, a blue glass bead and three coins of Nero. The second burial also contained a handled flagon and a platter with fragments of a jar and the remains of a bronze pin. Roman burial finds remain rare throughout Norfolk and these discoveries at Stanley Avenue thus have a significance considerably greater than their number.

A burial found at Woodlands Park, Dereham Road, in 1861 was reported by one John Wodderspoon to his friend T. Barton in a letter dated 10 December of that year. After thanking Barton for a brace of pheasants, he went on to say that he had …

> a few waifs and strays for you in the Archaeological line … You saw of course that
> workmen found what I believe to be a Roman interment in lead … the body was either
> a youth or female – the teeth, some of which I brought away, very beautiful …

It is likely that the discovery was third or fourth century in date. It consisted of a female skeleton in an unsoldered lead coffin with remains of another skeleton close by. Both the Stanley Avenue and Dereham Road discoveries were close to Holmestreet Way.

Other than these burials, evidence for Romano-British occupation is sparse, unlike that for the reuse of Roman material, much of it probably from Caistor. Roman bricks are built into the fabric of the Norman cathedral, while probable Romano-British rotary querns were discovered in 1948 reused as building material for eighteenth-century houses above the city ditch at Barn Road. Pottery sherds and coins are found scattered throughout the city, including coins of Claudius II, Aurelian and Diocletian from the corner of Dove Street and the Market Place, close to the probable line of the north-to-south Roman road. Such finds often cause problems of interpretation; it is likely that some of the exotic Roman coinage from the city arrived as souvenirs brought home by men of the Royal Norfolk Regiment in the nineteenth century.

Compared to a Roman settlement site, however, the material from Norwich is scanty. Evidence for the centuries immediately succeeding the Roman period is also thin. An Early Saxon cremation cemetery of fifth- to sixth-century date was discovered at Eade Road, north of the later city wall, in about May 1898. A man named Pike recovered an urn reputedly of fifth-century type and fragments of others; further finds, including a square-headed brooch, were found in July the same year. Apart from the brooch (which passed to the Castle Museum), the discoveries were dispersed (the urn going to the British Museum).

A fragment of cremation urn was also recovered in the early 1970s during underpinning of the chancel wall of the church of St Michael at Plea in the heart of the city. Although isolated, this discovery is of interest given the later importance of the church as a leet court and possible moot. A few similar sherds are also known from the area of the Norwich School within the Cathedral Close.

None of this amounts to sufficient evidence to suggest that any activity before the eighth century (at the earliest) can be regarded as 'proto-urban' (that is, a precursor to the establishment of the town). Furthermore, within the area of the greater city, evidence is not that much more prolific although work in 2001 at Bowthorpe has recorded three or four Early Saxon sunken-featured buildngs and post-hole structures. The most striking results came from excavation at Harford Farm, south of the city on the line of the Southern Bypass (1989-90), which uncovered a graveyard of probable seventh-century date with grave goods which seem to reflect an increasing level of affluence within the Norwich area (*colour*

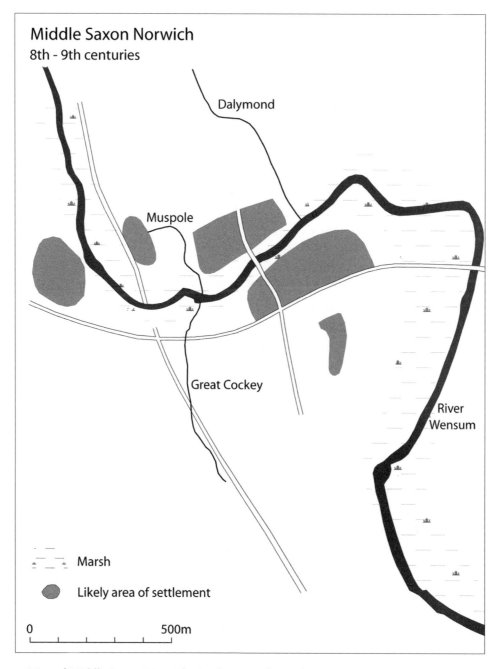

Middle Saxon Norwich
8th - 9th centuries

Dalymond

Muspole

Great Cockey

River
Wensum

‐ ‐ ‐ Marsh

Likely area of settlement

0   500m

7 Map of Middle Saxon Norwich (Sarah Leppard/David Dobson)

8 Excavation through the City Wall at Barn Road in 1952 (Provenance unknown)

9 Excavations on Fishergate 2005 (NAU Archaeology)

plate 2). The discoveries were made on the hill overlooking the site of Caistor Roman town to the south and the later medieval city of Norwich to the north. The cemetery may represent part of a gradual shift in emphasis northwards, away from the Yare-Tas valley and towards the Wensum-Yare valley, but it does not present evidence for an early urban existence.

ANGLIAN OR MIDDLE SAXON OCCUPATION

It is not until the eighth century that it becomes possible to suggest that proto-urban settlements were beginning to appear in the Wensum valley. These probably formed the earliest nuclei of the area that became the medieval city. The evidence for even these, however, remains sparse. It has therefore been a major objective of recent work to make this evidence less equivocal and rough patterns of occupation are beginning to appear.

Archaeological work concentrated initially upon the plotting of finds, predominantly those of pottery fragments but also of other artefacts, in order to produce distribution maps of eighth-century Anglian or Middle Saxon material from across the city (the latter term has traditionally been used for the period in East Anglian Norwich and so is used here). While such maps are necessarily subject to variables (for instance, nearly all of the material was located in 'secondary' contexts – that is it had been dumped within landfill or otherwise disturbed, rather than discarded where it was used – and quantities of data are necessarily only available from sites where fieldwork has taken place) it does nevertheless become possible to suggest areas of the city where concentrations of finds occur (a recent attempt at such plotting, for instance, implying a concentration of activity on the gravel terrace south of the Wensum and north of the later Cathedral Close).

These areas can be compared with place-name evidence as many early street and other names in Norwich can be shown to be Middle Saxon in origin. Examples include Westwick (as in Westwick Street), Coslany (as in St Michael Coslany), Conesford (Anglo-Scandinavian but based on an earlier formation and used in Conesford [now King] Street) and even Norwic (or Norwich). From here it is possible to predict probable areas of settlement and draw up a hypothetical model of the earliest settlement pattern which can then be tested by excavation and watching briefs.

The amount of information recovered remains relatively low but it is now possible to suggest that an early hypothesis, that Norwich 'nucleated' from a number of small discrete settlements, is probably incorrect. It is more likely that early settlement took account of the geography of the river valley, with settlement growing up along both banks of the Wensum above the well-drained

10 Sceat from
Fishergate 2005 (NAU
Archaeology)

gravel terraces. Evidence comes from 'Westwick', in the western part of the
historic core where pottery was located in excavation at low-lying Barn Road in
1952 and was the first of Middle Saxon date to be found in Norwich. Further
west, recent work at Wensum Street in 2001 seems to have revealed part of a
Middle Saxon building on the edge of the terrace, although excavation was
confined to a small trench and it was impossible to recover a plan. This structure
lies within the river edge concentration noted above but a further concentration
of Middle Saxon finds (including a sceat or coin and a disc brooch) has also
been made further downstream on Rose Lane while Middle Saxon pottery was
found on King Street in 1997. Any of these discoveries could have formed part
of 'Conesford'.

North of the river, it has been suggested that 'Coslany' may have stood at the
southern end of Oak Street although considerable recent excavation in the area
ahead of housing has failed to locate Middle Saxon occupation. 'Northwic' is the
most difficult settlement to locate within later Norwich because it eventually gave
its name to the whole area of the city. Some commentators maintain that it would
have been synonymous with Conesford and therefore stood somewhere in the
vicinity of the Cathedral Close; excavation in the 1980s, however, suggested that
a more probable location lay to the north of the river. This work, on Fishergate
in 1985, recovered considerable quantities of pottery sherds and other artefacts
of Middle Saxon date. While low compared to early towns such as Ipswich (and
many field-walked rural sites), the total of over 160 sherds remains large in a

Norwich context. The excavation produced more Middle Saxon material than all the previous excavations in the city combined, including a silver sceat. The deposits from which the finds were recovered were secondary, being rubbish infill next to the river, but they must represent the cleansing of occupation areas nearby.

More recent work at Fishergate in 2005 has produced further evidence of activity. As well as post-holes suggestive of a building, what seems to be a small purse-hoard of four further silver sceattas was found as well as a gold-plated imitation Merovingian tremissis. It seems likely therefore that the riverside here was home to at least seasonal commerce.

Not all Middle Saxon material has been recovered from the river margins; some pottery was located during the Castle Mall excavations on the flank of the Ber Street escarpment in 1989-91. However, it is notable that the greatest concentrations of pottery (from Fishergate, Barn Road and Rose Lane) are all from riverine sites while the major place-names (Northwic, Westwic, Conesford and Coslany) can all be associated with the river or with river crossings.

Early churches can be presumed within these proto-urban settlements and the sites of two such buildings can be postulated although, as yet, evidence has not been found to prove Middle Saxon origins. One of these is St Michael-at-Plea, already mentioned as the site of fragments from an Early Saxon urn and which, as St Michael *Motstow* or 'meeting place near the market', could have developed at an early period on an existing sacred site. It stands next to the east-to-west Roman road which runs from here down the east side of the Great Cockey valley before crossing the water and forming a crossroads with the north-to-south road at the church of St Gregory. This early dedication is given to a parish from which four other parishes (SS Laurence, Margaret, Swithin and Benedict) had been cut out by the eleventh century. It too may therefore be an early foundation.

Archaeological evidence, albeit slim, does exist for early development of a third church, also on the south bank of the river Wensum. This is the church of St Martin-at-Palace where excavation in 1987 uncovered post-pits for two timber buildings, one of which cut a burial, the radiocarbon date for which cannot be later than Middle Saxon. St Martin lies within the concentration of material noted from the south bank and the discoveries here thus tend to emphasise probable ribbon development along the river in the eighth century.

Topographically, however, the area north of the river either side of Fyebridge Street (and including Fishergate) can be suggested as the most likely location for an emerging urban centre. Unfortunately, it remains an area which has received relatively little archaeological attention, partly due to the lack of redevelopment in recent years as most rebuilding took place either before or shortly after the Second World War. There is sufficient general evidence, however, to postulate early significance.

Fishergate itself runs eastward from Fyebridge Street, the latter named from the most important medieval river crossing and possibly reflecting an earlier

Roman crossing. West of Fyebridge Street is a further street, Colegate, which extends, like Fishergate, along the north bank of the river. Both Fishergate and Colegate run towards streams (the Dalymond and the Muspole respectively) which could have acted as boundaries for nascent settlement. Early documentary references to the Spitaldike, immediately east of the Dalymond and north of the eastern arm of Fishergate, refer to it as the boundary of the borough.

Fyebridge Street runs northward (as Magdalen Street) towards Stump Cross, a fork in the road lost since construction of the Inner Relief Ring Road in 1974 (the area immediately north of this was known by the early name of *Mereholt* – 'boundary wood'). Listed buildings line both sides of Magdalen Street (as on much of Colegate) and it has thus remained largely immune to archaeological excavation. The potential of this main axial route and its two riverine side streets as the site of an important Middle Saxon settlement is thus untested but, as will be seen, it appears that this north bank area was developed as a fortified enclosure in the early tenth century, implying the probability of emerging importance, if not pre-eminence, at an earlier date.

It is clear that Norwich in general was no Ipswich or Hamwic (Southampton) at this period, the archaeological evidence, such as it is, merely pointing to a gradually developing urban community. The economic base of such a community is unclear but there are hints of trade. The 1985 and 2005 Fishergate discoveries of sceattas, a temissis (albeit a probable forgery) and pottery sherds from the Rhineland are indicative of this, as is similar pottery located at Barn Road 30 years earlier. It is interesting that the Rose Lane pottery finds were made next to the site of the church of St Vedast (or SS Vaast and Amand, two Flemish saints). This church is almost certainly of later, if still pre-Conquest, origin but the dedication to St Amand of Maastricht, a sixth-century Flemish saint, may be indicative of earlier trade contact with the Low Countries.

To date, there remains insufficient evidence to suggest whether parts of the settlement, on either bank of the river, were planned or merely grew up organically. With the possible exceptions of the fragmentary features from Wensum Street and Fishergate, remains of buildings have yet to be located. Other churches may date from this period (examples as disparate as St Michael Coslany, St Etheldreda and St John de Sepulchre have all been suggested) but none can be proven to be Middle Saxon in origin.

The apparent situation of ribbon development on both banks of the river probably continued into the ninth century. It seems clear, however, that thereafter a developing social and economic impetus led to the transformation of settlement into a more dynamic whole by the early eleventh century at the latest, and probably by the tenth century. It is not known where this impetus found its genesis but the incursion of the Danes into East Anglia during the third quarter of the ninth century seems a likely source.

THE ANGLO-SCANDINAVIAN BOROUGH

The Danes effectively conquered East Anglia after the defeat and murder of the East Anglian king, Edmund, in 870. While a decade of fighting across southern England was to follow, culminating in Danish defeat at the Battle of Edington against Alfred in 878 and the Treaty of Wedmore, it is subsequently recorded in the *Anglo-Saxon Chronicle* that, in 880, the Danish host 'went from Cirencester into East Anglia, and occupied the land, and shared it out'. Occupation must, in large part, have taken the form, of rural settlement, but the Danes also congregated in towns, as is known in the East Midlands with the Five Danish Boroughs of Nottingham, Derby, Lincoln, Leicester and Stamford. No mention is made of towns in Norfolk in this period, except that the Danish host wintered in Thetford in 870. It seems probable from a variety of evidence, however, that Norwich was becoming increasingly significant as an urban centre.

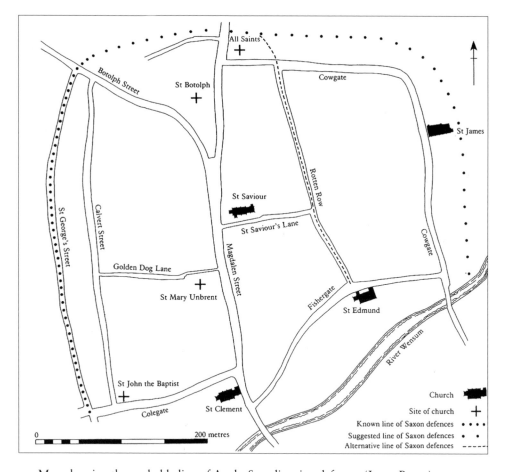

11 Map showing the probable line of Anglo-Scandinavian defences (Jayne Bown)

Norwich retains a rich and important inheritance which clearly dates from Danish occupation of the site. The most obvious evidence of this is that of place-names and street-names with Danish formations (such as Fisher*gate* and Potter*gate* – the streets of the fishermen and the potters) which were common in medieval Norwich. Many of these are known to have been coined as late as the fourteenth century (Westlegate) but they clearly reflect a considerable Anglo-Scandinavian heritage.

Most such names are related to streets but occasionally other locations can also be seen to have a name with a Danish origin. The royal, and subsequently episcopal, manor of Thorpe to the east of the city is a Danish formation ('new settlement') while the area of *Cowholme* (ultimately part of the Cathedral Close) means 'water meadow' or 'flat ground' from the old Danish word 'holm'. The importance of Thorpe, which included land west of the river Wensum (such as Cowholme) as well as east, to the development of Norwich was to be considerable.

Church dedications also suggest Danish influence. The Viking Saint Olaf (or Olave) was not martyred until 1030 but there were nevertheless two churches dedicated to him in Norwich, emphasising the residual importance of the Danish community in the eleventh century. In addition, it seems probable that the church of St Clement Fybriggate was a Danish foundation. St Clement is a most interesting parish. The extant building is predominantly a late medieval structure but the extent of the parish was once great, occupying large areas of the city both within and beyond the walls and possibly part of the early manor of Tokethorpe (from the Scandinavian personal name 'Toki' and 'thorpe'). Analysis of the medieval tithe pattern indicates that a number of the other parishes on the north bank of the river Wensum were either created by being carved out of St Clement's parish, two-thirds of their tithes being passed on to the mother church, or that St Clement was imposed upon them, perhaps by a Conquest-period individual who gave his name to the Tokethorpe manor.

Only some 50 or so pre-Reformation dedications to St Clement are known and a number of these are located in notable Anglo-Scandinavian towns – Ipswich, Cambridge and London are examples. St Clement was a popular saint in the Scandinavian lands – the cathedral at Aarhus is dedicated to him – and he was the patron saint of sailors, frequently being depicted with his anchor. A characteristic location of churches to St Clement in towns is near the river at the main river crossing, as in Cambridge and Huntingdon and also in Norwich.

The location of St Clement Fybriggate, in the heart of the area probably known as Northwic and close to significant excavations of early material (on Fishergate in 1985, where recovered artefacts included a linen-smoother of 'Viking' date, and in 2005), suggest that the centre of Anglo-Scandinavian activity in Norwich may have been on the north bank of the river Wensum, the Danes co-occupying that part of the growing city which was apparently most densely occupied by the

12 View of the Calvert Street
excavations 1989 (NAU
Archaeology)

Anglo-Saxons. Archaeological evidence remains thin but there is some support
for this assertion in the known location of a defensive ditch and bank which
encircled this area, probably from the early tenth century.

The existence of such a defensive system was first suggested by topographical
analysis of the street pattern of Norwich north of the river. This revealed
interesting features. The alignment of St George's Street (historically Gildengate)
runs northward from the river until it meets Botolph Street (largely lost after
1974). This alignment is paralleled by Calvert Street (Snailgate) immediately to
the east, both streets being continued in curving property boundaries north of
Botolph Street to effect a junction with the principal north-to-south route of
Magdalen Street (Fyebridgegate). East of Magdalen Street, the line of Cowgate
runs eastward until it curves south to the river.

The effect of these alignments is to suggest a D-shaped enclosure on the north
bank of the river. Excavation in the 1970s and again in 1989-90 on either side
of St George's Street revealed a ditch with the remains of a defensive bank
on its eastern side. This ditch had been re-cut twice and was infilled in the

twelfth century. Dating of its construction is difficult (a radiocarbon date for one excavation suggests only some time in the tenth century) but comparison with other enclosures would imply strongly that the earthwork is an Anglo-Scandinavian enclosure. Such defensive earthworks are known from Ipswich (where excavations in the 1980s suggested a construction of *c*.912), Repton, Bedford and, most famously, Hedeby or Haithabu, the great Danish emporium on the Baltic.

The extent of the enclosure east of Magdalen Street has yet to be confirmed by excavation. Work in 1992 on the north-to-south part of Cowgate (now Whitefriars) has demonstrated that the street here is a post-Conquest creation, with deposits previously thought to be ditch-fills being, most probably, infilling of low-lying land next to the river. It currently seems likely that any return to the river of a defensive alignment would be along Peacock Street (formerly Rattenrowe). This would take advantage of natural protection from the course of the Dalymond stream which flowed to the river here and would also make sense of early references to the edge of the borough. The western side of the defended enclosure would have been protected by the Muspole, an area of low-lying marshy ground. Again, such topographical positioning between protective streams or low-lying ground parallels other Anglo-Scandinavian enclosures such as Bedford and Lincoln where streams mark the flanks of defended areas.

The defences would have been pierced by two streets. Botolph Street and Magdalen Street, requiring gates. Topographical analysis can suggest the location of these as well. Botolph Street is named after St Botolph's church (which disappeared in the sixteenth century), a dedication frequently given to churches close to gateways in urban defences (such as the churches of St Botolph Aldersgate,

13 Borre-style brooch from the Anglia Television excavation of 1979 (NAU Archaeology)

Aldgate, Billingsgate and Bishopsgate in London or St Botolph in Cambridge). St Botolph Norwich was not close to the later medieval city wall but was adjacent to the smaller, earlier, defended enclosure. Similarly, the position of the gateway at Magdalen Street is marked by the location of the church of All Saints (also lost in the sixteenth century although burials were located by excavation in 2006). Here the church was so close that it can be suggested that it was originally part of the gate structure, as is known from examples at Canterbury.

The north bank settlement did not exist in isolation. Excavation in the last 20 years south of the river Wensum has also provided increasing evidence of Anglo-Scandinavian occupation. It is notable for instance, that the bulk of the diagnostically 'Viking' artefacts to be recovered from the city all have provenances on the south bank. These include tenth-century Borre-style brooches found in excavations near Rose Avenue, a cross fragment of tenth-century interlace recovered from the site of the church of St Vedast on Rose Lane, a Ringerike-style bronze mount from St Martin-at-Palace Plain and, as late as the beginning of the twelfth century, an early capital for the cathedral decorated with an intricate Urnes-style interlace.

Similarly, excavations beneath the site of the Franciscan friary in 1992/93 revealed perhaps the most unusual Viking artefact from Norwich. This is a half-*eyrir* lead weight bearing the name of Alfred but most probably a Danish copy of a Canterbury die of coins of Alfred the Great. It is possible that this weight could have been used in the manufacture of coins in Anglo-Scandinavian Norwich, emphasising the importance of the growing town, although it is likely that any such activity took place in the early 880s.

A further discovery on the south bank was made in 1999 although here the location was west of the Great Cockey in an area previously thought to be

14 Coins of Aethelstan (Norfolk Museums & Archaeology Service)

outside early areas of settlement. Excavations at the site of the Millennium Library off Bethel Street uncovered a Viking gold ingot (*colour plate 3*), litharge and fragments of a ceramic crucible with traces of gold. The implication is clear: goldworking seems to have been taking place, perhaps in a location away from combustible buildings.

Although an increasing number of pre-1066 buildings have now been excavated, only one has been located whereby it can be suggested that it dates to the later ninth or early tenth centuries. This too lay beneath the Franciscan friary site where an industrial building of post-hole construction was discovered with an imitation coin of Alfred the Great (dated 887-9 and struck by a moneyer called Wigmund) in one of the post-holes, and a complete (if fractured) Thetford-type vessel (from the tenth to the twelfth centuries) on the floor.

It is probable that at least one bridge connected the settlements and industrial activities on the south bank with the defended enclosure north of the river. A causeway constructed of wooden piles, across the riverside marsh and the Wensum itself, was discovered in 1896 during works to construct a sewer at Fye Bridge. The alignment of this causeway was checked by further excavation in 1974 and again in 1999 when part of a pile was recovered. This pile retained all its sapwood and bark, encouraging hopes of a good dendrochronological date, but unfortunately it was not possible to match the timber and it remains, for now, undated. Although a coin of either William the Conqueror or William Rufus was found within the causeway, its topographical position suggests strongly that the structure dates from the tenth century.

While the absence of documentation hinders understanding of the extent of Viking Norwich, it is possible to imply the nature of the growing town from other evidence. This settlement was clearly no Jorvik, or even a Stamford or Derby, but it was probably beginning to thrive. The greatest concentration of activity was almost certainly in the vicinity of St Clement Fybriggate but the diversity of activity is now becoming clearer through excavation. High-status activity such as coin- and goldworking existed alongside high-quality manufacture such as bronzeworking. Status symbols certainly existed in the growing borough: as an example, a late ninth-century sword was recovered from the river Wensum in about 1854.

Perhaps, however, the greatest contribution of the Danes was to define Norwich as a burh or borough; this too is not clear from documentation but can be inferred from later activity. East Anglia fell to the Saxon king Edward the Elder in 917, Norwich thus returning to the English orbit. His son, Aethelstan (924-39), codified the practice of placing mints in towns, seeking to locate them within defended areas. Norwich, with its enclosure, was a logical town for just such a mint and, in the 930s, there is, at last, a positive indication of the settlement's growing status; among mint signatures of Aethelstan's coinage appear, for the first time, that of *Norvic* or Norwich.

2

THE LATE SAXON
(OR ANGLO-SCANDINAVIAN)
TOWN

Aethelstan's instructions concerning mints were included in a set of decrees issued at Grateley, Hampshire, in *c*.935. These not only specified the locations of mints but sought to regulate the function of towns as trading centres. It is likely that the king was merely regularising developing practice but the implication for Norwich, with its mint established by the second quarter of the tenth century, is that it was acting as just such a market centre. Moreover, it is probable that it was also developing as a centre of administration within East Anglia.

The settlement may have been gaining recognition as a growing town of importance but this is still not reflected in extant documentary sources. No mention of Norwich is made until the 980s when the *Liber Eliensis* or Book of Ely records that Abbot Brithnoth of Ely, when buying land in Cambridge, was assured by all there 'that Cambridge and Norwich and Ipswich and Thetford were of such liberty and dignity that if anyone bought land there he did not need witnesses'. This implies a well-established town and suggests that the settlement had been growing in status for the previous 50 years. The material evidence is, however, difficult to locate.

Most of the archaeological work of the last 35 years, and most work at any previous time, has been undertaken on the south bank of the river Wensum. This has frequently uncovered material of eleventh-century date but, until recently, it was only rarely that any occupation could be demonstrated to be unequivocally of the tenth century. It is clear that there was tenth-century activity but nothing apparently of the intensity to suggest the growing town implied by both mint status and the *Liber Eliensis* reference. Excavation at sites such as Castle Mall, below the Franciscan friary, Palace Street and King Street, all on the south bank, have now produced evidence for tenth-century occupation. The accumulating data suggests a growing and diverse community, furnished with churches, a regular street system and industrial activity. This is all encouraging but it does not assist understanding of the fortified enclosure on the north bank, with its probable site of the mint. Work here has been much more patchy, with a consequent difficulty in tracing development.

THE NORTH BANK

The absence of archaeological data from the north bank is mainly the result of a relative lack of recent development and thus appropriate excavation. However, this dearth is complemented historically by the relative distance of the area from the Castle Museum. For much of the quarter century after the Second World War, casual finds uncovered by development were recorded by staff of the Castle Museum (usually during lunch hour). Distance clearly inhibits such casual recording, an inhibition amplified by the instance that, until the late 1970s, no member of staff lived to the north of the city and thus did not pass development sites to and from work! In consequence, finds from this area were recorded infrequently.

Modern development control procedures now ensure a more systematic appraisal of building works throughout the city but it will still take time before there is a substantially greater data-set for the north bank area. The 1985 Fishergate excavation produced a corpus of pottery which suggested considerable tenth-century activity in the vicinity but, despite more recent work on this street (notably in 2005), there has been hardly any other work within the defended enclosure. Excavations have been undertaken off Calvert Street, to the east in 1990 and to the west in 1998, and also on Cowgate in 1999. All three of these, however, were adjacent to the defences (and, in the case of the Cowgate site, quite probably outside them) and thus at the fringes of settlement: little tenth-century activity was observed in 1990; the 1998 site was heavily disturbed by early medieval quarry pits; and the earliest activity that could be determined in 1999 was late eleventh- or early twelfth-century in date. Other north bank work has certainly been outside the Anglo-Scandinavian defences. Excavations at Alms Lane in 1976 located eleventh-century ironworking; work at Coslany Street in 1996 again encountered eleventh-century activity as the earliest occupation; and further eleventh-century occupation was located at Oak Street in 2000. Limited work at Fishergate in 1999, west of the 1985 and 2008 excavations and probably beyond the defences, did not reach early deposits while it was only possible to dig one or two small test-pits beneath the otherwise extensive excavations of the Carmelite friary in 2002.

This is all somewhat dispiriting although it is important to note that it has not been possible to examine deposits in key areas, namely Magdalen Street south of Stump Cross, Colegate east of St George's Street and, apart from one small site in 2005 (which located pre-Conquest material), Fishergate north of the road. Development opportunities here will continue to be rare given the wealth of the historic built environment and any which do arise, and for which appropriate access and resources can be obtained, should add considerably to current understanding of the early city and its importance.

The tenth-century importance of Norwich is, of course, evident from the information given to Abbot Brithnoth when he visited Cambridge. It is an importance which probably had a growing international reputation given the location of Norwich on the east coast and which perhaps led to the event mentioned in the second documentary reference to the city, an event somewhat more dramatic than the abbot's excursion. The *Anglo-Saxon Chronicle*, in its first reference to Norwich, states that in 1004, King Sweyn of Denmark 'came with his fleet to Norwich and completely burned and ravaged the borough'.

As with so much of the early history of Norwich, the site of this disaster is unknown. With occupation evident on both banks of the river, destruction could have been wrought throughout the settlement. It is possible, however, that the north bank suffered particularly badly. This part of the city is known in later documentation as *in combusto* ('in the burnt area'). While the city no doubt suffered numerous fires in the Middle Ages, and it would be too much to assert that *in combusto* refers to Sweyn's attack, the possibility that it does do so must exist. It is interesting that, of all the many churches of the medieval city, only two had fire references in suffixes to their dedications: the churches of St Mary *Combuste* and St Margaret in *Combusto*. Both are now lost (St Mary amalgamated with St Saviour in the sixteenth century and St Margaret ultimately with St Paul) but both stood on Magdalen Street. St Margaret is late, probably founded about 1100, but St Mary may well have dated to the pre-Conquest period; it stood at the corner of Magdalen Street and Golden Dog Lane in the heart of the defended enclosure.

Sweyn's attack may have been devastating but it does not seem to have arrested the growth of Norwich. On the contrary, growth thereafter seems to have been little short of spectacular. Documentation remains very scanty (a reference to Cnut or Canute at a battle near Norwich in 1014, but possibly referring to his activities with his father in 1004, and two wills are all that are known) but all other evidence suggests a burgeoning community. Norwich may have been 'completely burned and ravaged' in 1004 but, by 1066, it had at least 25 churches (and possibly as many as 40) with a population estimated between 5000 and 10,000 people.

THE SOUTH BANK

The bulk of this population certainly lived south of the river at the Conquest and may have already done so by 1004. Tenth-century evidence from excavations on King Street at the Ben Burgess site in 1999, similar evidence at Castle Mall between 1989 and 1991 and also from Palace Street in 2000 indicate occupation from the river in the north to Mountergate in the south and from the Great

15 Walrus ivory pectoral cross
(Victoria & Albert Museum)

Cockey in the west to the river marshes in the east. Indeed, the area was well-bounded by water or low-lying marshy ground, save to the south where the steep slopes of the Ber Street escarpment provided dry-shod access. Here, however, work off King Street to the south of Stepping Lane, also in 2000, uncovered a ditch, four metres wide and two metres deep, which perhaps formed a boundary to the settlement. Hardly substantial enough to be defensive and with no sign of a revetment, dating is also problematical. A tenth-century date seems likely, possibly late in the century when delimitation of the south bank town might have created a 'double *burh*' either side of the river at Norwich, as was created earlier at places such as Hertford. Part of a further ditch was seen in the courtyard of Cinema City off St Andrew's Hill in 2004, cut through the chalk hill and quite probably part of the same boundary system.

Within the area bounded by the Stepping Lane and St Andrew's Hill ditches, there is considerable topographical, ecclesiastical and archaeological evidence for the growing tenth- and eleventh-century settlement. Analysis of this development, however, is complicated by the imposition of the castle and cathedral precincts in the Norman period and that of the Franciscan friary in the thirteenth century, all of which destroyed existing topography. Nevertheless, sufficient evidence survives, above ground in the built topographic environment, below ground in archaeological deposits, and by inference from later documentation to enable an assessment of the morphology of the Anglo-Saxon town, an assessment which continues to improve with ongoing research.

The centre of this developing urban area was Tombland, the site of the market place with the place-name meaning 'empty' or 'open' space. It was a location which boasted a house belonging to the bishop at its northern end (where the Maid's Head hotel now stands) and, reputedly, the 'palace' of the Earls of East Anglia to the south. The richest church in the borough, that of St Michael Tombland, was located here; the building was destroyed during the initial construction of the Cathedral Close in the 1090s but the discovery of a walrus ivory pectoral cross (the finest piece of pre-Conquest art from the city) during excavation of subterranean lavatories in 1878 probably indicates its location.

Tombland itself survives and stands astride a relict pre-Conquest urban landscape. Streets to the north, south and, particularly, to the west can be suggested as elements within the Late Saxon or Anglo-Scandinavian town. Recent work also renders it possible to reconstruct the alignments of other streets or lanes now lost beneath later topography. Most strikingly, a metalled road was uncovered beneath the Franciscan friary in 1992, the metalling largely dating to the thirteenth century but its alignment almost certainly established before the Conquest (*colour plate 8*). Early and heavy use had eroded the surface to form a hollow way, hoof impressions being recovered from the mud at its base. The northward extension of this lane seems to have been uncovered by excavations west of the north-to-south part of St Faith's Lane in 2008 and it is likely that it extended further north to pass in front of the west face of the later cathedral church, thereafter linking with the still extant Pigg Lane and the river. A second north-to-south road was postulated in the 1970s, running from St Vedast Street northward beneath the transepts of the cathedral to meet *Bichil*, also at the river. Work at Palace Street in 2000 suggests that a third north-to-south lane, between these other two, remained fossilised in part as Beckwith's Yard, now preserved within a new housing development.

These three north-to-south routes, together with the King Street/Tombland line, were crossed by at least three – and probably more – east-to-west routes. The greatest of these was the Roman road described in Chapter 1 (p.23). It was supplemented by the Rose Lane route and a probable road linking Elm Hill to *Bichil*. In addition, two minor lanes are suggested by the east-to-west parts of St Faith's Lane and rights of way west of them, Mountergate probably acted as

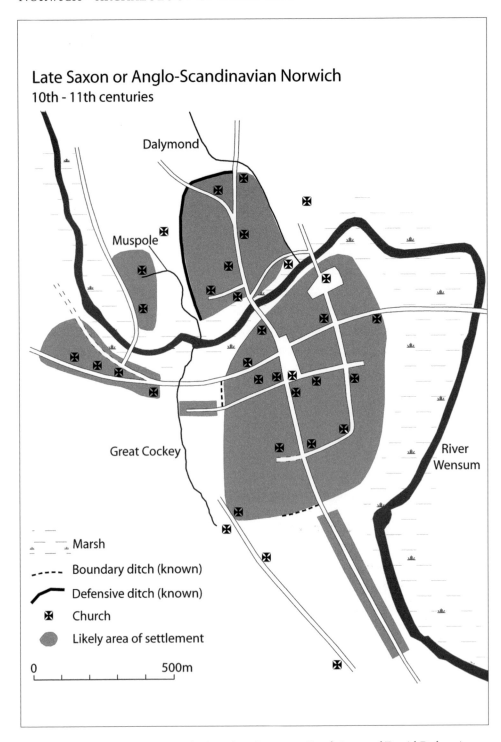

Late Saxon or Anglo-Scandinavian Norwich
10th - 11th centuries

Dalymond

Muspole

Great Cockey

River
Wensum

- Marsh
- Boundary ditch (known)
- Defensive ditch (known)
- Church
- Likely area of settlement

0   500m

16 Plan of the Late Saxon or Anglo-Scandinavian town (Sarah Leppard/David Dobson)

a curving route along the edge of the marsh to the south (a gravel road surface was uncovered here in 1998), and a further, somewhat curious, gravel road surface was discovered at an angle of some 45° to the emerging grid beneath the cathedral refectory in 2001.

Another route could be expected to develop along the south bank of the river. Here excavation has shown considerable infilling from the edge of the gravel terrace for a distance of some 60m north to the river, culminating in construction of a timber revetment, the timber for which was felled in the summer of 1146. The resulting quay was probably only the last in a progressive series of quays, the earliest of which almost certainly dates to the Anglo-Scandinavian period. Similar revetting, of a braid in the river Wensum upstream at Coslany Street, was observed in excavation in 1996 while small-scale excavation off Mountergate in 1998 uncovered the edge of a small cockey revetted in the eleventh century with reused fragments of a boat.

In total, occupation on the south bank probably occupied some 50ha (125 acres), although the density of such occupation was undoubtedly patchy. However, the reconstructed urban plan has considerable regularity and may possibly be the result of conscious and ambitious town planning. A context for such deliberate plantation would be the interest of important magnates; it can be noted from Domesday Book that the king, the earl, the bishop, the abbots of Bury and Ely as well as the sister of the bishop, are all known to have held land in Norwich before the Conquest. These magnates between them controlled all the burgesses of the settlement in 1066, implying considerable oligarchical control.

The extent and shape of the town by the eleventh century is most eloquently expressed in its churches. Eight are recorded by name as existing before 1066 (All Saints, Christ Church, St Laurence, St Martin, St Mary [in the Marsh], St Michael [Tombland], SS Simon and Jude, and St Sepulchre). With the possible exception of All Saints which is probably a reference to All Saints Fybriggate rather than the church on Westlegate, all the named churches are on the south bank. Interestingly, two lie outside the main settlement area. St Sepulchre stands on the south end of the Roman road of Ber Street, some 500m south of the ditch discovered in 2000 and overlooking both the Wensum and Yare river valleys. St Laurence stands west of the Great Cockey. It was in existence by 1038 and, certainly in the later Middle Ages but probably also from the beginning, paid part of its tithes to St Gregory. The implication of the tithe payment, which it is known mirrors the situation with the other three churches in the area, those of SS Margaret, Swithin and Benedict, is that Norwich had acquired an eleventh-century suburb, carved out of the pre-existing parish of St Gregory.

Suburban activity is hinted at elsewhere. The 1999 excavations at the Millennium Library site uncovered two ditches which suggest a road or lane, probably linking St Gregory along the southern crest of the cockey valley with the road south towards Thetford. In Heigham to the west of the historic core of Norwich, work in 2000 uncovered tenth- to eleventh-century pottery while on King Street, south of the Stepping Lane ditch, excavations at Dragon Hall and Cannon Wharf in 1997 both produced evidence of eleventh-century activity including timber structures. Moreover, the southern part of King Street also contained a further church dedicated to St Clement and another church dedicated to St Olaf, both probably pre-Conquest foundations and both implying a small riverside settlement in this area.

Churches other than those named in early documentation undoubtedly existed and can be suggested by architectural detail, dedication or excavation. This last has discovered (in 1979) a previously unrecorded timber church demolished to make way for the castle. The final, eleventh-century phase of this building, is an early example of a stave-type church, another indication of the importance of the Anglo-Scandinavian tradition in Norwich. Excavation of further burials both in 1979 and subsequently between 1989 and 1991 at Castle Mall suggests two, and possibly three, other lost and unrecorded pre-Conquest churches.

The density of probable Late Saxon or Anglo-Scandinavian churches is particularly apparent in the vicinity of Tombland and adjacent streets where

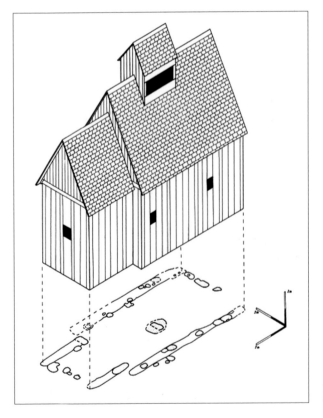

17 Plan and reconstruction of the eleventh-century timber church (NAU Archaeology)

many either stood or appear to have stood on street corners. Examples can be cited of the churches of St Mary the Less, St Michael-at-Pleas, St Peter Hungate and SS Simon and Jude of extant examples and probably St Cuthbert, St Ethelbert, St Mary-in-the Marsh, Christ Church, St Helen, St John the Evangelist and St Vedast of lost examples. Excavation in 1987 at the cathedral uncovered burials immediately west and below the north transept which probably indicate the location of Christ Church. Part of the later structure of the church of St Cuthbert was uncovered in commercial excavations in 1939 and burials in 1952. The graveyard extended northward to the market place on Tombland as was shown by further work in 1999 when another burial was uncovered in conversion works to 27-28 Tombland. The dedication to St Cuthbert is an unusual one in southern England and is paralleled by a similar example close to the market in Thetford.

This consistent positioning, with the two rich churches of St Michael Tombland and St Martin-at-Palace occupying central sites within open areas (Tombland and *Bichil* respectively), assists reconstruction of the pre-Conquest street pattern. It also enhances the possibility of deliberate planning of the borough.

CHURCH BUILDINGS AND GRAVEYARDS

The excavated timber church beneath the site of the castle was probably typical of the type of churches erected in Norwich in the eleventh century. The building is of unknown dedication and stood where offices for Anglia Television now stand. Excavation ahead of construction of these offices in 1979 uncovered the complete ground plan of a post-in-slot timber church with a rectangular nave and a square chancel. The building was furnished with a font (the soakaway for which was located) and possibly with a belfry (supported on a post set centrally within the nave). Graves were located around the building although not within it, consistent with Anglo-Saxon burial practice. The church was deliberately destroyed after the Norman Conquest, almost certainly to allow the construction of the north-east bailey of the castle.

Timber would have been the normal building material although some stone churches were probably in existence by the time of the Conquest. One such was probably the church of St Martin-at-Palace which was held by the bishop (Stigand) in 1066 and which, in the east wall of its chancel, has long-and-short work datable to the Conquest period. Excavation has also revealed characteristic Saxo-Norman flint, chalk and gravel foundations. The building was preceded by two earlier timber structures, one of these probably being furnished with at least some well-appointed graves. Fragments of a Lindsey-type limestone grave cover with interlace decoration, rare if not exceptional in East Anglia, were uncovered by the excavation.

Fragmentary long-and-short work is also visible in the east wall of St John Timberhill and pre-Conquest work has been claimed within other extant buildings such as St Gregory but the case remains to be proven. Excavated evidence for stone churches has proved as elusive although very few sites have been investigated; work on the bombed church of St Benedict in 1972 recovered probable pre-Conquest burials but no sign of a church, the earliest stone building post-dating 1066.

Graveyards, or parts of them, have been explored as at St John Timberhill in 1989 where it was possible to establish an early churchyard boundary on the north side of the church. Here, a curving ditch was shown to mark the edge of the early graveyard (although it may have been cut in the post-Conquest period). The graveyard bounded by the ditch went out of use in the fifteenth century (the church itself remains in use to this day) but the curve of the boundary was marked by buildings off an alleyway (Grout's Thoroughfare) until at least 1883.

The church at the Anglia Television site seems to have existed for only some 75 years. The graveyard was thus of particular importance because it contained

18 Lindsey-style grave cover
(NAU Archaeology)

individuals who were almost exclusively Anglo-Saxon or Anglo-Scandinavian without the possibility of mixing with burials of later date. Analysis of the skeletons, therefore, enabled a study of an essentially pre-Conquest population. The assemblage was small (only about 130 individuals as not all the graveyard was dug) but it showed that the people in this parish at least were poor and generally malnourished. Rickets was common amongst the child burials and the adults showed signs of having suffered similarly in youth. The skeletons of the adult males were particularly notable for the muscle strains evident in the bone, implying lives full of hard physical labour.

Burials uncovered as part of the Castle Mall excavations included a group of 189 individuals with perhaps one-fifth of these suffering from leprosy. It was possible to date one particular burial to between 930 and 1050 and to establish that the person interred was of Romani descent, easily the earliest known instance, being some five centuries before the first record of such people in the sixteenth century.

19 Skull showing pronounced sutures indicative of rickets (David Wicks)

DOMESTIC, INDUSTRIAL AND COMMERCIAL BUILDINGS

Few pre-Conquest buildings were recognised in Norwich prior to the 1980s. Excavation in 1981 on the riverside gravel terrace at St Martin-at-Palace Plain uncovered evidence for a number of timber structures. Two types were identified, the one built above discrete post-holes and the other above post-in-slot footings. The larger buildings appeared to have stood at right angles to the street with smaller structures parallel to the street at the rear (precision is difficult because complete ground plans could not be recovered due to destruction of the evidence by the construction of later buildings).

Infilling of the walls was probably effected with wattle-and-daub (some was found in one of the post-holes) and roofs could have been thatched. These timber structures may have been houses for domestic occupation but it is just as likely that they formed a type of warehouse or store as no evidence was found for domestic rubbish disposal. It is possible to visualise a small commercial community working next to the river, especially as fragments of similar structures were observed immediately downstream during excavations in 1972.

The problem of damage to archaeological deposits by development in later centuries is common to all towns where density of occupation has gradually increased. The survival of evidence for pre-Conquest buildings in Norwich as elsewhere is particularly rare as secular buildings were built of wood. Very little of the historic core of the city contains waterlogged deposits, which enhance the preservation of the wooden elements of buildings, and thus the archaeological clues to such buildings consist of fragile features such as infilled post-holes. Dense development over most of the last thousand years has ensured that much destruction of these features has taken place, leaving only tantalising fragments of building plans to suggest location, size and orientation.

These fragments have been seen on numerous excavations in the city, on both sides of the river (a notable example being located beneath the bank of the later medieval defences at Barn Road in 1954/55). The first complete ground plans of secular buildings, however, were recovered by excavations on the 2.4ha (6 acre) Castle Mall site between 1989 and 1991. While the forms of some 27 buildings have now been reconstructed from the complex excavated evidence, the ground plans of two structures in particular were very clear when excavated in late 1990. These were examples of a type of building which incorporated either cellars or, more probably, sunken floors, supplementing discrete post-hole and post-in-slot examples. Two similar buildings were also excavated between King Street and Rose Lane in 1992 and on Palace Street in 2006.

The sunken floor in each building was created by the excavation of a large straight-sided pit, sub-rectangular or square in the case of the four Norwich structures, perhaps to a depth of 1-2m (the full depth had been truncated at

Castle Mall by eighteenth- and nineteenth-century landscaping and, in the case of the buildings near King Street and Rose Lane, by thirteenth-century and later works for the Franciscan friary). Vertical posts were then set out at intervals around the base of the pit with horizontal planks behind the posts, between them and the pit sides. The posts and planks thus revetted the sides and created a small, subterranean room. The tops of the posts were probably jointed into a sill beam with the superstructure of the building rising out of the upper face of the beam, the implication being that these were simple timber-framed structures. The building near King Street was furnished with a hearth of re-used Roman bricks and it and the Rose Lane structure had ledges which may have served as bases for wooden benches.

These 'sunken-featured' buildings were probably used as craft workshops in a similar manner to examples known from other pre-Conquest urban sites, notably York. Excavation at King Street in 2001 recovered evidence for at least two buildings (one with daub walling) associated with antlerworking, while work in 1997 behind the later medieval Dragon Hall further south on King Street recorded buildings constructed with posts which were also probably used for craft activities, antlerworking again being one such occupation. One of the Palace Street buildings appears to have burnt down and excavation revealed a carbonised rolled-up fishing net within it.

At least one of these Dragon Hall site buildings used peat as a fuel and there was some evidence to suggest the division of tenement plots. Similarly, at Castle Mall, shallow linear ditches may have represented property boundaries and at least one boundary could be suggested from excavation at St Martin-at-Palace Plain in 1981. It is not yet possible, however, to argue convincingly for the survival of pre-Conquest property boundaries, through known medieval tenement patterns, to the complex post-medieval tenemental organisation which is now largely disappearing or has indeed disappeared.

Fragmentary evidence for eleventh-century timber buildings now exists from several parts of the city: excavations in the late 1990s onwards have uncovered post-holes, slots or surfaces at Cowgate, Oak Street, King Street, St Faith's Lane, beneath the refectory of the cathedral and at two sites on Palace Street, the 2006 excavation mentioned above and earlier work in 2000. This earlier Palace Street site was particularly striking: here, above tenth- and eleventh-century consolidation of the river foreshore, a succession of chalk-floored structures were excavated, furnished in one case with wickerwork walls between posts. The earliest such building dated to the eleventh century although renewal was maintained into the fourteenth century. Norwich was beginning to establish an infrastructure which would be long-lasting.

COMMERCIAL AND INDUSTRIAL ACTIVITY

The buildings excavated at the Palace Street site actually fronted the river. The Wensum was very much at the heart of this developing borough, serving a community which continued to occupy both riverbanks. The north bank was not deserted when spectacular growth became evident to the south although a decline to subordinate status must have set in, a decline made only too obvious by the name given to the medieval leet or administrative area of the north bank – *ultra aquam* or 'over the water', presumably away from what was now the centre of the settlement or the centres of administrative control (the post-Conquest castle, cathedral and Market Place/Tollhouse). River trade, however, probably maintained activity on Colegate and Fishergate.

Such trade certainly helped to develop areas to the south at places like St Martin-at-Palace Plain. Here, a gravel terrace at the northern edge of *Bichil* (bitch's hill or beak-like hill and first recorded at the end of the twelfth century), was consolidated by the dumping of animal dung, rubbish and straw, held in place by small wickerwork fences. The resulting surface or 'hard' next to the river would have been used to beach river craft, and probably the occasional seagoing vessel, for the loading and unloading of goods over the side. Excavation uncovered evidence for such surfaces upstream of Whitefriars Bridge in 1979 and downstream in 1981. The second, and larger, excavation also located evidence for boat-building in the form of timbers set into the gravel foreshore which probably formed the basis of frameworks for construction in a manner paralleled by discoveries in Schleswig, northern Germany.

Ships, of course, enabled international trade as much as local or coastal trade. Such trade is perhaps implied by the existence of the church of St Vedast which, as mentioned in Chapter 1, was originally dedicated to two Flemish saints, Vaast and Amand (Vedast was subsequently anglicised to St Faith). The church was demolished in the sixteenth century but its site may indicate the location of a small, pre-Conquest, Flemish community (there is another St Vedast off Cheapside in London). This would emphasise the growing commercial importance of Norwich, a borough now of considerable administrative significance for both secular and ecclesiastical powers and with an increasingly diverse economic base. The town was becoming a major market centre, trading in goods to its hinterland, the region and across the North Sea.

International trade was probably quite restricted although archaeological evidence has demonstrated eleventh-century contacts with Scandinavia, the Low Countries and the Rhineland. Regional and local trade was clearly much more important. The population of East Anglia, and particularly of eastern Norfolk, was remarkably dense by 1066 compared with much of the rest of lowland England. Unlike other southern shires, however, few towns had developed in Norfolk so that Norwich already dominated a rich agricultural area. Its remarkable growth must have owed much to this fortunate circumstance.

Providing products with which to trade, as well as ensuring the supply of materials with which to develop the settlement, meant that craft industries and other activities grew in number within Norwich. It seems possible that some industrial work included the heavy activity of quarrying. By the Middle Ages, the exploitation of quarries in and around Norwich was very great and it is likely that the tradition began in the pre-Conquest period, providing flint and lime mortar for the few stone churches as well as lime to spread on the town fields. It has been suggested that some of the adult males recovered from the graveyard at the Anglia Television site showed muscle strains and bone deficiencies consistent with that of poorly nourished miners.

The quarrying trade can only be surmised but there is increasing archaeological evidence for other industries such as the extraction of iron ore from the river gravels (as at Alms Lane in 1976 where excavations uncovered quarries for nodular ore or iron pan, roasting hearths and smelting furnaces), iron-smithing (St Faith's Lane 1997), ironworking (Oak Street 2000), comb-making (Fishergate 1985 and St Faith's Lane 1997) and antlerworking (King Street 1999). Among other craft industries, the strong Anglo-Scandinavian inheritance can be seen in Borre-style brooches, only three of which have been found in Norwich, all within 50m (165ft) of each other near Rose Avenue, implying a workshop in the locality. It is possible that other metalwork was also manufactured in the city, perhaps including the eleventh-century Ringerike-style mount from St Martin-at-Palace Plain which may have formed part of a saddle.

20 Andenne and Pingsdorf Ware (Brian Ayers)

The saddle itself, of course, would have been made of leather and evidence for leatherworking has also been found, particularly on riverside sites. Here shoemakers' and cobblers' waste indicate that the animals which were being brought into the borough were not slaughtered solely for their meat. Tanners must have existed to supply the leatherworkers and the finished items of shoes, clothing and utensils would have been sold back to the countryside as well as to the inhabitants of the borough.

Other industries can be recognised on the river margins. The retting of flax seems to have taken place at St Martin-at-Palace Plain where stakes driven into the gravel foreshore may have been used to tether the flax (flax seeds were recovered in soil samples taken during excavation in 1979). Woodworking can be observed in excavated archaeological material, such as the remains of an oak box with dovetailed or rabbetted joints or an ash core from the turning of a wooden bowl (also recovered in 1979). Analysis of timbers recovered from the waterfront suggests that coppicing was practised.

Another pre-Conquest industry which would have entailed considerable labour was that of potting. Evidence for this activity is now extensive. Kilns seem to have operated by the eleventh century along both sides of Bedford Street (historically Pottergate, 'the street of the potters') producing an earthenware pottery known as Thetford-type ware (large quantities of waster vessel fragments have been recorded in watching briefs and excavations over the last 30 years). Suitable clay existed in the Norwich area but not that close to Pottergate and it must have been imported.

The pottery industry produced a range of vessel types although the most common was the jar, followed by small lamps. The vessels were unglazed but occasionally decorated with rouletting or, in the case of spouted pitchers and large storage jars, with applied strips of clay thumbed to make a pattern. The kilns were pits cut into the ground, one of which was excavated in 1980. It was oval in shape with a stoke-pit and two pedestals within the main combustion chamber. Pots were stacked around these pedestals and the full kiln was probably roofed with turf.

Pottery produced in such kilns was distributed over a wide area, not just in Norwich where it occurs on all eleventh-century pre-Conquest sites, but also to much of the rest of East Anglia and other parts of eastern England. It may even have been traded across the North Sea; Thetford-type pottery found on the Bryggen excavations at Bergen in Norway may have been manufactured in Norwich (although there were also production centres in Ipswich and Thetford itself). Earlier commentators frequently confused the fabric with Roman material, leading to erroneous conclusions. The ware continued to be made in Norwich into the twelfth century.

Eleventh-century Norwich is thus gradually becoming more visible, mainly through the medium of archaeological excavation. It is possible that the

Right: 21 Excavated Thetford-type ware pottery kiln (Brian Ayers)

Below: 22 Cut-away reconstruction of Thetford-type ware pottery kiln (Susan G. White)

churches of St Martin-at-Palace and St John Timberhill contain work of Late Saxon date but largely the pre-Conquest borough survives only in the inherited topography and below-ground archaeology. These nevertheless contain sufficient information to suggest a vibrant and rapidly growing town with a diverse economic base (affluent in some sectors as seen in artefacts such as a buckle frame and plate decorated with animal heads found at St Faith's Lane in 1997) and an increasingly complex social organisation.

The borough of Norwich was Anglo-Scandinavian as much as it was Anglo-Saxon. Its Nordic tradition is probably best exemplified by the pre-1066 obligation on the citizens to provide the king with a bear, information lying within the Norman Domesday Book, a post-Conquest document which allows a glimpse of Norwich at the time of the Battle of Hastings. The glimpse thus afforded complements the evidence of the topography and archaeology, providing a framework for the late pre-Conquest discoveries and a background for the great changes which the Norman Conquest brought to the settlement. Anglo-Saxon Norwich had come to dominate its local area by the mid-eleventh century; the Normans would extend this local importance to regional supremacy.

23 Bronze strap-end (Ryszard Hajdul)

3

NORMAN NORWICH – THE SECULAR TOWN

The Norman impact upon Norwich was extraordinary, even by the standards of that extraordinarily energetic people. Within a generation following 1066, the basic urban topography had been changed more utterly than would be effected by any subsequent change prior to the twentieth century. The Normans seem to have found a thriving and growing borough but they stamped their authority upon the settlement with such thoroughness that the modern geography of the historic core is fundamentally an Anglo-Norman and not just an Anglo-Scandinavian construct.

The Normans influenced every sphere of life. While it is generally true that, at a base cultural level, it remains difficult (if not impossible) to differentiate Anglo-Scandinavian occupation of the mid-eleventh century from that of the early Norman period (a difficulty underlined by the discovery at Castle Mall in 1989 of a bowl in a fabric usually dated to about 1100 but with stamped decoration of apparently earlier date), the establishment of major institutions such as the castle and the cathedral ensured a domination of the borough by the new regime. Norman influence was indeed so pervasive between 1066 and the end of the twelfth century that it is easier to discuss the development of Norwich at this time in two parts: secular and ecclesiastical.

The single most important source for an initial understanding of Norwich in the years immediately after the Battle of Hastings is that provided by the Normans themselves, the entry concerning Norwich in the Domesday Book of 1086. Norwich is fortunate in that its entry is in Little Domesday, the volume covering Eastern England which appears to be an earlier stage in the compilation process that went to produce the Great Domesday. Entries in the latter seem to be edited versions of more detailed data, data which therefore survives for Norwich. This both assists and complicates because, as always with historical research, the more data that is available, the more questions can be asked.

Domesday Book paints a picture of a town fallen on hard times by 1086. A population comprising some 1320 burgesses in 1066 had dropped to one of 655 burgesses. It seems likely that the effects of the Conquest and its aftermath had reduced the financial status of some of the 1066 burgesses to that of bordar or smallholder class (there were 480 of these in 1086 but none were mentioned for

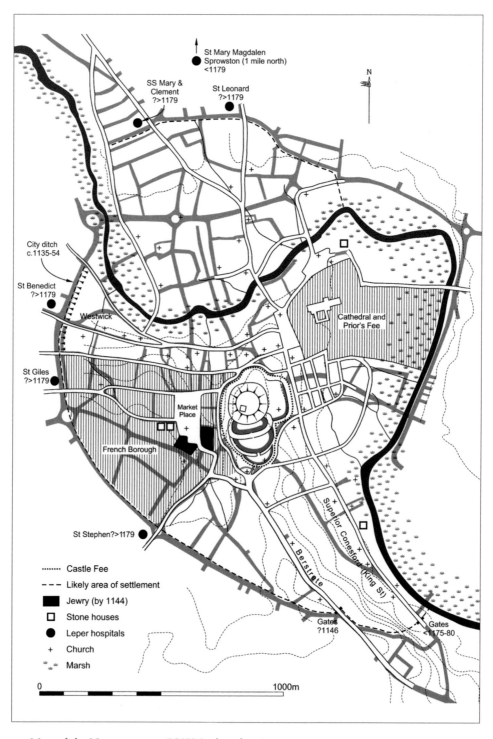

24 Map of the Norman town (NAU Archaeology)

1066) while 22 burgesses had quit the borough and fled to Beccles in Suffolk. The document complains that 'those fleeing and the others remaining have been utterly devastated partly because of Earl R(alph)'s forfeitures [Ralph was Earl of Norfolk and Suffolk until 1075 when he rebelled unsuccessfully against the Crown], partly because of fires, partly because of the King's tax, partly by Waleran [who held the borough in fee and farmed the tax]'.

This makes gloomy reading (and possibly represents compilation by a surviving member of the pre-Conquest administration) but it is also clear from the account that the infrastructure of the borough was already diverse. Between 25 and 40 churches seem to have been in existence by 1066 and at least one further foundation is recorded before 1075. A castle was defensible by 1075 and a new borough had been laid out to the west of the Anglo-Saxon town. Devastation in the years leading to 1086 had clearly been considerable (and would be followed by more disruption in the 1090s) but the establishment of institutions such as the castle would have a profound, and largely beneficial, impact upon the settlement's fortunes.

NORWICH CASTLE

The castle, a royal rather than a baronial foundation, was probably under construction before the end of the 1060s as an earthwork and timber fortification. The provision of necessary space entailed the demolition of at least 98 houses which were now *in occupatione castelli* ('occupied by the castle') according to Domesday Book. This clearance may have involved the demolition of at least two churches as well. One of these, excavated in 1979, has been mentioned above; the other lay beneath the rampart of the south bailey and part of its graveyard was excavated in 1989.

Work on the castle was sufficiently far advanced by 1075 for the fortress to withstand a siege when the Constable, Ralph de Guader, rebelled against the king (a hoard of William I pennies, discovered in London Street in 1972, may have been hidden at the time of the siege). The castle was invested by Lanfranc, Archbishop of Canterbury, who wrote an account to the Conqueror in Normandy when the garrison surrendered. This, probably the earliest English battle dispatch, read that:

> ... Norwich Castle is surrendered and the Britons [Bretons] who were in it and had lands in the English land, life being granted to them with limbs have sworn that within forty days they will go from your Kingdom ... In the same Castle have remained Bishop Geoffrey, W. de Warenna, Robert Malet and 300 men in armour with them, with Crossbowmen and many artificers of machines. All noise of wars (God pitying) is quiet in the English land ...

The detail 'with limbs' was important for the besieged: rebellious Bretons at Winchester in the same year were maimed and blinded. The respite for the Bretons of Norwich was brief as the unforgiving Conqueror punished them at Christmas 1075:

> Some of them were blinded,
> Some of them were banished,
> Some were brought to shame.
> So all traitors to the king
> Were laid low.

There has been considerable excavation of the castle precinct in the last 25 years (*colour plate 5*) although it would be too much to expect this work to reveal direct evidence for the siege. However, the combined results of investigations within the north-east bailey (1973 and 1979), the major excavations of the south bailey and part of the extramural castle fee to the south-west (1989-1991) (*colour plate 6*), work on the southern defences (1998), evaluation within part of the eastern fee (2000), exploration of the castle bridge (1989-1993) and sectioning of the castle mound (1999-2001), together with many other minor observations, have greatly increased understanding of the development of the fortress.

The castle at Norwich covered an area of some 9.3ha (23 acres), the fortification in place by 1075 probably already extending across that area ultimately occupied by the extant great mound or motte and two baileys or enclosures. Excavation in 1999 in advance of the insertion of modern lifts into the southern and eastern flanks of the mound indicates that the earliest earthwork consisted of a smaller mound occupying the area now largely surmounted by the great keep or *donjon*, possibly with an embanked entrance to the north-east. The early mound was erected on an existing hill at the northern end of the Ber Street escarpment, overlooking the river to the north and east. It was created by heaping upcast from a deep ditch, either destroying or burying pre-Conquest occupation surfaces in the process, the ditch serving to separate the mound from the hill and bailey to the south. Timber buildings and ramparts were presumably erected above the earthworks.

Evidence that the original castle included a smaller mound subsequently extended to form the existing great mound, can be found by interpretation of observations made in 1968 during construction of museum stores. The 1960s was such a dire decade for archaeology that even a museum building could be erected, on an internationally important site, without prior excavation, but surviving photographs seem to illustrate an early mound beneath the later stone keep.

The 1968 work was not the only earlier excavation into the mound. The hill was cut back to the east for construction of the Shirehall in 1822, a partial section was excavated in 1906 for the Shirehall extension, and widening of the street now called Castle Meadow to the west in the late 1920s led to the building of the extant brick-and-flint retaining wall in this location. Records of the 1906 work in particular, together with more recent excavations, demonstrate that the mound was both steeper and with a deeper ditch than appears today.

The early Norman castle was transformed before the end of the eleventh century with massive re-modelling of the defences and the construction of major stone features. Excavations in 1999 uncovered evidence for the construction of a large earth bank to the east of the early mound followed by some occupation on the inner slope of this bank, but soon thereafter deposition of a thick layer of re-deposited chalk, dumped within the bank to bring levels up to that of the early motte, thereby creating an enlarged mound. At the same time, new outer fortifications of defensive banks and ditches were constructed around the southern bailey. Work in 1998 uncovered the terminal of one of these ditches, indicating that the south gate was approached across a causeway on uncut earth. By 1100 the castle was an exceptional fortress with the largest mound in England and two fortified baileys or enclosures (the north-east bailey was known as Castle Meadow and almost certainly providing grazing for the herds and flocks of the garrison).

It is now possible to suggest the general disposition of the defences for the baileys albeit still with a degree of inference as much of the north-east bailey

25 East exterior elevation of the keep of Norwich Castle by William Wilkins (Norfolk Museums & Archaeology Service)

remains unclear, as does the eastern arm of the south bailey. Nevertheless, the increase in knowledge is remarkable given that landscaping in 1738, and again in 1862, had so thoroughly levelled the castle earthworks that the alignment of the ditches was lost and reconstructions as late as 1975, using all the available non-archaeological evidence, made considerable errors of plotting.

Within the re-modelled fortress, stone buildings were erected. The dearth of good building stone in Norfolk meant that the castle defences were always substantially of earth and timber but major stone monuments were nevertheless constructed, notably those of the keep, the bridge, and the now lost south gate and medieval Shirehall. Of the two surviving monuments, both were heavily re-faced in the nineteenth century, necessary procedures but, on both occasions, ones handled in an unfortunate manner with the effect of obscuring, until very recently, both the importance and the distinctiveness of the structures.

Norwich Castle keep is an extraordinary building although much mutilated on the interior by the destruction of nearly all its internal partition walls, and on the exterior by its re-facing. This last was undertaken in 1834-9 and substituted Bath stone for earlier Caen and Barnack, re-faced areas of Norman flintwork with ashlar, reduced the number of merlons on the battlements, added a corbel table beneath the battlements, and scored-out fake joints on the new facing stone. However, it is clear from late eighteenth-century surveys that the 1830s

26 Norwich Castle keep showing re-facing of 1830s (Brian Ayers)

work did replicate as far as possible the profusion of exterior blind arcading for which the building is widely noted.

The Norman building accounts for the keep are not known to exist. As a result, dating of the structure has generally proceeded by analogy with similar buildings. Initial construction has been traditionally attributed to the reign of Henry I (1100-35), largely on the grounds of stylistic comparison with tower keeps such as that at Falaise in Normandy, but also by noting that the masons' marks within the building are paralleled at the better-documented cathedral. Recently, however, it has been argued convincingly that the structure could date from as early as 1095. A critique of the design aesthetic, together with careful analysis of the building process itself, has determined that the building not only underwent changes of plan during construction but that its design concept is more akin to project initiation in the reign of William Rufus (1087-1100).

Detailed survey and analysis has demonstrated that the keep was planned in considerable detail using strict mathematical formulae. On the exterior, these not only determined the relationships of the pilaster buttresses to the plain wall lengths between them but also dictated the heights of string courses and provided a visual external demarcation of the internal spaces of the building. The mouldings of the external decoration are related to the proportional system which dictated the positions of the various rows of blind arcading.

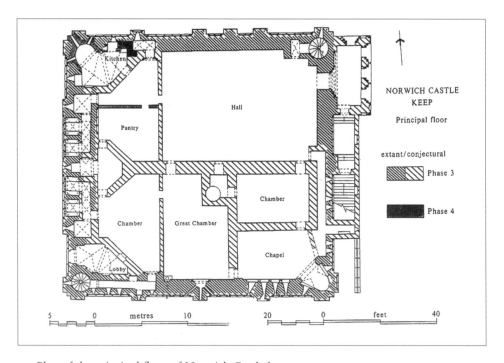

27 Plan of the principal floor of Norwich Castle keep

The mathematical system persists on the interior although here it is also supported by a quality of sculpture which is unsurpassed in any other secular building of its date. The (now demolished) approach tower led to a landing (still extant above a rib vault) before a great, richly decorated doorway with three orders of arches and carvings which depict scenes from the hunt and mythological characters and creatures. This doorway led to a large first-floor hall, south of which, through a spine wall which divided the structure into two, lay a chapel (with further sculpture on the chancel arch capitals) and a sumptuous chamber with a fireplace (again with sculptured capitals) and remains of a wash-basin set into the south wall.

The chapel seems to have been an afterthought, inserted during the course of construction when a small kitchen was also added above a spiral stair which had reached principal floor level but was never completed. The keep is also furnished with an extensive suite of latrines, making the building suitable to act as a large audience chamber as much as a fortified residence. It is palatial in scope, designed to act as the seat of the king in the affluent eastern counties or of his representative in his absence.

After the keep, the most spectacular surviving monument at the castle is the bridge to the mound. This structure is probably contemporary with the keep although the earliest reference to a stone bridge concerns *repairs* in 1173. It too was re-faced in the early nineteenth century but excavations in 1990 and 1992 have demonstrated that it is substantially Norman. It is formed of two abutments, the southern one of which has a buried plinth of nine courses of chamfered Caen stone beneath a faced wall also of Caen stone. Above, remains of a medieval gravel road surface survive beneath the modern tarmac.

The northern abutment has an infilled void, probably to accommodate the drawbridge of an upper gatehouse, remains of which stood on the bridge until the eighteenth century. Linking the abutments are two arches of flint and mortar, both substantially medieval with evidence of a removable timber roadway between them. The timber was subsequently replaced, presumably by a vault, which was itself renewed in brick in 1830. The underside of the keystone is inscribed 'May 19 1830', a most helpful aid to the archaeologist!

A further gatehouse stood at the foot of the bridge, the foundations of which form the footings of the present nineteenth-century structure. Beyond, it is likely that there was yet another gatehouse. Massive remains of the flint and mortar structure of this later building, together with dressings of limestone, were uncovered in the 1989-1991 excavations.

The castle, being a royal foundation, was outside the jurisdiction of the borough. It occupied its own 'liberty' or 'fee' and the land of the fee extended beyond the castle defences on all sides, most notably to the west. Here the ditch of the castle is now followed by a road (confusingly named Castle Meadow,

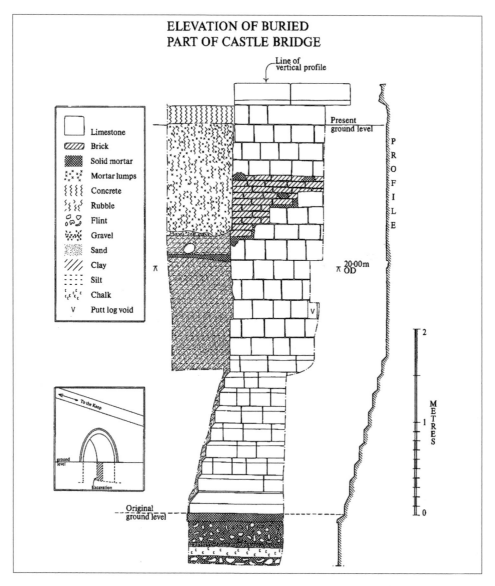

ELEVATION OF BURIED
PART OF CASTLE BRIDGE

28 Elevation and profile of the excavated base of the south abutment to the Castle Bridge showing the Caen stone facings and the plinth of nine chamfered risers, now beneath the Castle Gardens (Hoste Spalding)

'borrowing' the place-name from the north-east bailey). West of this, however, is a street which runs concentrically with the ditch, now divided into London Street, Castle Street and Back of the Inns. This formed the boundary to the Fee, the boundary perhaps being marked by posts with plaques bearing the royal arms set upon them. Four such plaques were discovered in 1964, each pierced by several small nail holes. The fee boundary itself may have been marked here and

29 Plaque with the royal arms
(NAU Archaeology)

elsewhere by a ditch, as off Timberhill where excavation in 1989 revealed such a feature. It is possible that small but deep excavation off Castle Street in 1999 also encountered the infilled ditch.

THE FRENCH BOROUGH

The establishment of the castle was initially the responsibility of Earl Ralph. He also founded, with the king, a borough for their Norman-French compatriots. This borough, referred to in Domesday Book as for the 'Franci de Norwic', lay to the west of the castle on land which had probably served as open fields for the pre-Conquest Anglo-Scandinavian town. This much is implied by the name 'Mancroft' subsequently applied to the whole area. Mancroft means '(ge)maene croft' or 'common enclosure', 'common land'. As noted above, however, excavation in 1999 uncovered a more complex situation, the location being used for some industrial activity and being crossed by one or more roads. The generally open field state of the area can nevertheless be suggested by the curious alignment of St Peter Street which may derive its distinctive reverse 'S' pattern from development above the headland of previously agricultural land.

The church of St Peter Mancroft, by the later Middle Ages the most important church in the city, is probably the 'certain church' which was also founded by Earl Ralph. The church was almost certainly constructed of stone from the beginning although it was entirely rebuilt in the later Middle Ages. A recent appraisal of the extant building, however, has determined the sequence of rebuilding and thus, by extension, the probable plan of the pre-existing structure. A central tower is postulated with short transept arms or transeptal chapels, a chancel and a nave. This is the Romanesque structure likely to have dominated the borough.

The French Borough was laid out around a large rectangular market place with two main streets leading westward, Upper Newport (now Bethel Street) and Lower Newport (St Giles Street). Two other churches, St Giles and St Stephen, were also founded. Tenements were created, visible to the west of the Market Place on the 1883 Ordnance Survey map or in air photographs of the early twentieth century, as narrow strips running back from the St Peter's Street frontage. These tenements were destroyed by the construction of City Hall in 1938 but similar ones still exist to the east off Gentleman's Walk.

Until 1999 hardly any excavation had taken place in the French Borough but destruction by fire of the 1960s Central Library in 1994 provided the opportunity for archaeological work ahead of the construction of a new Millennium Library. The site lay immediately to the west of St Peter Mancroft and St Peter's Street and, perhaps unsurprisingly, late eleventh-century tenement boundaries were located. However, once again, the situation proved more complex as, in the twelfth century, it is clear that the Bethel Street frontage became more important, substantial stone houses being constructed here, perhaps with an associated change in property boundaries. The somewhat slight remains of the buildings add to a growing corpus of stone house discoveries in Norwich and will be discussed below.

30 Norwich Market Place from the tower of St Peter Mancroft (NAU Archaeology)

THE JEWRY

The eastern edge of the borough was probably marked by the line of the Great Cockey stream, the eastern bank of this stream being the boundary of the castle fee. Between the castle and the French Borough, and partly within the borough, was an area largely occupied as a Jewish Quarter. Predominantly grouped in and around Saddlegate (now White Lion Street) and the Haymarket, the Jews of Norwich formed one of the most important such communities in England.

There is no evidence that Jews lived in Norwich, or indeed England, before the Conquest. A community was established in Norwich by 1144 and may date from 1135 while a man called 'Isaac' is mentioned in Domesday Book. The concentration of Jews near the castle (although not all lived here) must have been for royal protection and is paralleled in other towns.

The Jewish community in Norwich is one that is comparatively well-documented. A third of the English medieval Jewish deeds in Hebrew and almost half of those in Latin refer to Norwich. From these, it was possible in 1967 to reconstruct and publish the broad tenement pattern of the Jewry. Archaeologically, however, there is as yet little diagnostic evidence for the Jewish community. Material recovered on the site of the Littlewoods store (between the Market and the castle fee) in 1962 included a stone column with characteristic Norman tooling which may have come from the synagogue (known to have stood hereabouts) and which was either burnt down in 1286 or demolished in 1290. A bronze bowl (the 'Bodleian Bowl'), now in Oxford, was discovered in Norfolk in or before 1696. It is inscribed with a rabbinical inscription and is thought to have originated with the Norwich community. The greatest surviving Jewish artefact, however, is the so-called Jurnet's house on King Street.

Jurnet's Hall or the Music House is a three-storey building which stands on the east side of King Street next to the river Wensum (about 500m [1650ft] south-east of the main area of Jewish settlement). It consists of a chamber block at right-angles to the street frontage, built of flint with limestone dressings. The ground floor is divided by a wall into two rooms, the front one of which has a two-bay quadripartite limestone vault while that to the rear has groin vaults in three bays. An internal stair gave access to the first floor from the rear room. Access from the exterior was to the south where windows were set into narrow embrasures. Dating of the chamber block is problematical but it could have been built c.1140. Around 1175 it was augmented by an aisled hall which was built to the south, blocking outside light to the windows. This hall had an eastern arcade of which part of a pier survives with details identical to those on the Infirmary at the cathedral (a watching brief in 1996, following un-notified commercial excavation, *may* have recorded part of a further range to this building complex but damage to the exposed wall fabric and associated deposits was too great for this to be determined).

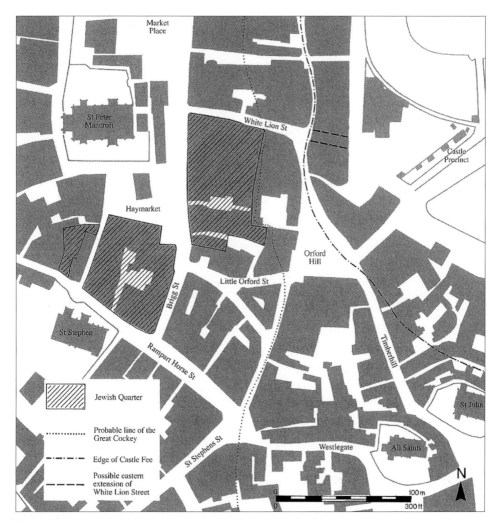

31 Detail of the 1883 Ordnance Survey map annotated to show the medieval Jewish Quarter (Ordnance Survey/Karen Guffogg)

The building is the oldest surviving house in the city and may have been occupied by Jurnet, a wealthy Jewish financier. It was certainly owned by his son, Isaac, who also used the river to trade as he was licensed to extend his staith behind the building in 1225. Isaac's role as a financier ensured that he appears frequently in Exchequer records and one of these, dated 1233, contains a caricature of him together with his agent Mosse Mokke and a woman called Avegaye. This, perhaps the earliest caricature in England, depicts Isaac as the three-headed king of Norwich, its anti-semitic point nevertheless demonstrating his great importance.

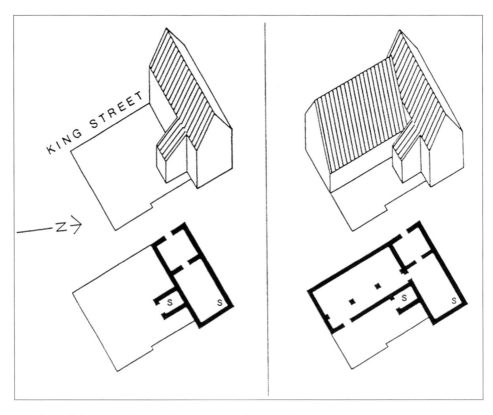

32 Plans of the Music House, King Street (Robert Smith)

33 Anti-Semitic cartoon on an Exchequer document of 1232-33 depicting Isaac, the son of Jurnet, and other Norwich Jews (Public Record Office)

BUILDINGS

The house of Jurnet and Isaac was not the only stone house in Norwich. Recent documentary research, supplementing work first undertaken in the 1980s, has identified 18 such buildings but others certainly existed. Such references all occur in post-Norman documents but are most likely to refer to twelfth- and thirteenth-century buildings. They indicate that stone buildings, which clearly represented a considerable investment of capital, tended to be constructed in four (generally affluent) principal areas: around the Market Place; along the waterfront on King Street; on Tombland (an eroded capital survives in the cellars of the Maid's Head Hotel); and along the waterfront north of the cathedral.

Substantial remains of a stone building were discovered in 1981 in the last of the above areas. Excavations at St Martin-at-Palace Plain on the site of the new Magistrates' Courts unexpectedly revealed a twelfth-century building of flint rubble with limestone dressings. It stands (the ruin is preserved beneath the Courts in a modern basement) at right-angles to the street frontage with internal measurements of 13.5m by 6.7m (44ft by 22ft). Cut into the hill, ground-floor access was afforded from the street to a first-floor hall below which was a partly cellared basement. This was served with two doorways and three window openings and seems to have been roofed in timber. At the northern (river) end of the building is a latrine turret, designed to allow the removal of effluent from the upper floor(s).

The nearest parallel, both in terms of style and distance, for this excavated structure is the Music House and the buildings are approximately contemporary. The excavated example was almost certainly a monastic property, attached to the Benedictine priory of the cathedral. Rents were payable to the Cellarer of the cathedral, implying that the building may have been used as a victualling warehouse for the monastery. It was destroyed in the late thirteenth century, perhaps in 1272 when the townspeople rioted against the priory.

More recently, excavated evidence has been located for other stone buildings. Demolition debris of a twelfth-century stone house was uncovered in 1998 behind Dragon Hall on King Street while a thirteenth-century stone building was excavated on the same site (it was owned by the Abbot of Woburn in 1289 whose predecessors may have been responsible for its construction). Opposite Dragon Hall, excavation in 2000 uncovered a further stone building, with a latrine arch of dressed stone in Romanesque style although this may have been re-used. In addition, as mentioned above, evidence for two further houses was discovered at the Millennium Library site. These buildings had been thoroughly robbed of their stone but rammed gravel foundations indicated their positions and size. It is possible that these houses were associated with a limekiln excavated on the same site (*colour plate 11*). This pit, filled with chalk, oxidised lime and charcoal, is the only medieval example known from the city.

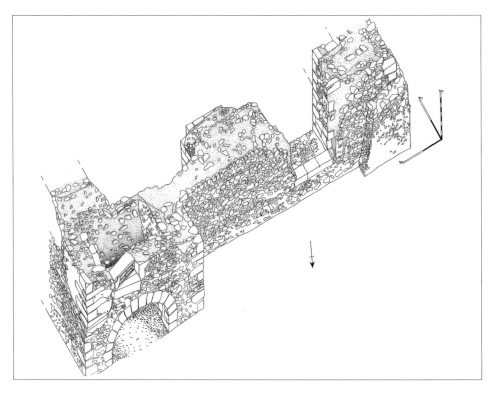

34 Axonometric projection of excavated twelfth-century stone building (Philip Williams)

35 Detail of west wall of excavated stone building (Brian Ayers)

Stone houses were, of course, the exception in Norman Norwich where most buildings continued to be constructed of wood or even earth. The earliest examples of clay-walled houses date to the twelfth century. Such buildings rarely appear in documents but instead are recognised by excavation. They were either constructed with cob (consisting of clay puddled in water with chopped straw and other aggregates such as chalk and flint which was layered between shutters to make walls) or clay lump (where clay was formed into regular blocks with moulds). Timber buildings located off Timberhill at Castle Mall in 1989 were eleventh or twelfth century in date and elements of Norman timber structures were located on King Street in 1999 and on Palace Street in 2000.

URBAN DEVELOPMENT

Norman occupation of Norwich clearly had a dramatic effect when institutions such as the castle were established above pre-existing properties. Similar if less dramatic effects were seen at Bethel Street in the twelfth century when early Norman property boundaries were changed. Radical alteration to the urban landscape has also been observed elsewhere such as on King Street where property boundaries were altered on the Dragon Hall site in the late twelfth century or at St Martin-at-Palace Plain in the third quarter of the twelfth century. Here construction of the stone building took place on land acquired by the bishop in 1106. The 1981 excavation revealed that the site had been occupied by earlier timber buildings but, following clearance, the area seems to have been laid out afresh, the stone building standing within a tenement plot some 60ft (18m) wide. Analysis of property boundaries on the 1883 Ordnance Survey map, together with a thirteenth-century list of the prior's landgable (rents on land), would suggest that the tenement of the stone building was only one of a number of similar tenements, each about 60ft wide. Each paid 1d in landgable except for a more narrow property next to St Martin's bridge some 30ft wide which paid a halfpenny. Interestingly, a similar linked system of property size and rents is paralleled at King's Lynn (also ecclesiastical land) where the 'new land' was laid out in the twelfth century with tenement size related closely to rental income. Urban growth in the Norman period was clearly planned with care.

Other plantation took place north of the river Wensum in the second quarter of the twelfth century. Here, on land west of Tolthorp Lane (subsequently Rattenrowe and Peacock Street) Eborard, the second Bishop of Norwich, established a small community around the church and hospital of St Paul on land belonging to his manor of Thorpe. Until recently, it was an area which had not been subject to any major excavation. However, following work in both 1992 and 2002, together with other small-scale observations, it seems evident that the site was largely one of marginal land which needed considerable dumping of infilling deposits to ensure its viability. The episcopal initiative can hardly be called a success; the area was always to remain peripheral to the centres of activity in the growing city.

Planned expansion such as that around St Paul's church was complemented by more ad hoc expansion to both the north and south. Linear development along the line of Magdalen Street north of the Anglo-Scandinavian defences seems to have taken place at the end of the eleventh and the beginning of the twelfth century with the church of St Margaret in Combusto, the most northerly church within the later walled city, being founded about 1100. Other churches to the north-west, such as St Augustine and St Martin-at-Oak, may have been founded at about the same time. This expansion was probably encouraged by the gradual decay, and ultimate removal, of the Anglo-Scandinavian defensive bank and ditch. These were perhaps outmoded before 1066 but would certainly have ceased to have any official function in the aftermath of the Conquest. Excavations at Alms Lane and Calvert Street indicate that the ditch was filled with rubbish or backfilled with its rampart around 1100 with extramural settlement, albeit housing the urban poor, being established by the twelfth century. Impoverished housing was accompanied by a continuation of impoverished industrial activity; ironworking seems to have persisted on Oak Street throughout this period.

South of the river, development extended along King Street in the early twelfth century. The area has only recently been subject to relatively detailed excavation but this is now indicating that essentially suburban activity in the eleventh century had merged with the growing city to form part of the urban core 100 years later. Twelfth-century buildings such as those at the Music House (Jurnet's Hall) or on the Dragon Hall site are obvious high-status examples but activity was certainly present as far south as St Olaf's parish where a lined well or cesspit was recorded in trial excavations in 1997 (the site also produced good-quality Romanesque stonework, probably demolition debris from a church such as that of St Olaf). Further work a little to the north in 2003 uncovered riverside revetments which incorporated the remains of four twelfth-century boats. Norman expansion may even be evident in churches of apparent early date such as St Julian (with its round tower and 'basket' window) which could be a late eleventh-century foundation although it is possible that the churches of St Clement and St Etheldreda do indicate the location of pre-Conquest settlement.

Expansion was not possible to the east due to the location of the river and its marsh (and the land of the bishop) but, to the west, development continued. As an example, pre-Conquest growth along St Benedict's Street seems to have been supplemented by development of the river marsh off Westwick Street in the twelfth century. Excavation in 1972 uncovered tenement boundaries established at this date and which persisted into the twentieth century. Gradual encroachment on the river is characteristic of much of the central part of the city in this period, with infilling of the river margins occurring on both banks.

The growth of settlement on either side of the river probably necessitated the construction of additional bridges. It was noted above that Fye Bridge was probably built before the Conquest although the earliest known documentary reference is 1130-33. St Martin's or Whitefriars Bridge was constructed by 1106 and may be pre-Conquest in origin but could also have been erected to link the cathedral precinct to episcopal land north of the river. By the end of the twelfth century a third bridge existed, linking Oak Street with Coslany Street in the western part of the city. This bridge was referred to in the thirteenth century as 'duos pontes de Koselanye', probably because the bridge was in two parts, using an island in the river as a midway stage. The place-name 'Coslany' refers to such an island which became attached to the north bank by infilling in later centuries.

TRADE AND INDUSTRY

Riverside colonisation seems to have been undertaken primarily for industrial reasons. Excavations at St Martin-at-Palace Plain located deposits of the first half of the twelfth century with considerable quantities of *Reseda luteola* seeds (dyer's rocket) being found in the soil samples, providing evidence for the nearby use of the plant in the dyeing process. Norwich was beginning to establish itself as a cloth-finishing city, probably working on cloth produced in the surrounding countryside although there is a curious reference in a French chronicle to the sack of Norwich in 1174 by the Flemings when the settlement failed to defend itself adequately as Norwich men were 'for the most part ... weavers, they know not to bear arms in knightly wise'. Weavers would have needed wool to make cloth and excavation in 1992 on Whitefriars recovered an early wool comb of bone, the first such to be found in the city.

Tanning and skinning were other riverside trades, exploiting the hides of the increasing numbers of animals brought into the city for slaughter. Skinners probably worked on Mountergate and there is an early oblique reference to the trade in accounts of the life of St William of Norwich, the boy saint ostensibly murdered by the Jews about 1144. William was apprenticed to a skinner and therefore is the earliest recorded apprentice in English history.

Other industries along the river included hornworking (where cattle horns were steeped in pits full of urine and water to remove the tine; examples have been located on Pitt Street and on Fishergate). Hornworking also took place next to the streams or cockeys which flowed through the town; horn waste was recovered from the Midland Bank site on London Street next to the Great Cockey. Clenchbolts recovered from the Dragon Hall site on King Street suggest the possibility of boat-building or boat-repairing. Further south, a perforated polygonal ash object found at Cannon Wharf is interpreted as a block from ship's rigging. It is possible that iron for these boats may have been sourced locally; there is excavated evidence for iron extraction from river gravels in the Oak Street area. Gravel itself was excavated wherever possible for surfacing the streets and yards of the growing town. Archaeological investigations off Rose Lane and King Street in the early 1990s, off Calvert Street in 1998, at Timberhill and off Cattle Market Street in 2000 all uncovered quarry pits (the Calvert Street examples containing quantities of waste from ironworking). Mills were recorded in Domesday Book and, by the twelfth century, are known to have stood in the western part of the city (the Westwick or Appleyard mills are recorded from 1175 and the 'Calk milnes' from about 1186).

Evidence for daily life in Norman Norwich continues to be located by excavation. The production of pottery in the town seems to have ceased by the mid-twelfth century but supplies of pottery were imported from the immediate hinterland and further afield. Commercial sites and affluent locations such as the castle reveal fragments of high-quality Andenne Ware from the Low Countries or Pingsdorf, a red-painted pottery, from the Rhineland (a wine merchant from Cologne is mentioned in a document of 1144). Other continental imports include hone stones from Norway and quern stones from Germany while occasional discoveries of pottery from Beauvais and Rouen suggest that the Norman Conquest brought an expansion to trade links which hitherto seem to have largely centred on the Rhine basin and the Baltic.

ENVIRONMENTAL EVIDENCE

Less obvious imports were plants, introduced to England through ports such as Norwich. Analysis of microscopic seeds from Whitefriars has revealed the earliest known instances in the country of pot marigold and hops. Part of a walnut was also found, the earliest known post-Roman instance of the nut in England. Such discoveries help to develop a picture of a society which was both growing and outward-looking.

Scientific analysis of microscopic flora and fauna, as well as the study of larger environmental ecofacts such as fish bone, also enables a clearer understanding of everyday life. Well-preserved organic deposits of late eleventh- and early twelfth-century date, excavated in 1981 near the river, provided excellent evidence for the content of midden or cess deposits. Cereal cleansing waste, food refuse and floor sweepings of bracken and heather were all identified as well as fruits such as sloe, bullace, plum, cherry, apple, strawberry, medlar, grape and elderberry. Fish remains were dominated by marine species, notably herring and cod. Animal bones consisted mainly of cattle, sheep and pig although cats and dogs (presumably domestic pets but hounds were most probably kept as well) were also found as well as occasional deer and hare. Diet, therefore, seems to have been as varied as local resources allowed.

Norwich by the end of the twelfth century was a considerably larger settlement than that at the Conquest. It had been augmented by development on marginal land and along the river, notably to the south. Much of this development remains to be explored archaeologically (the Norman waterfront is only one area of great significance as yet largely untested by the trowel) but the broad trend of development seems clear. Norwich had consolidated its position as the most important settlement in the county, and indeed the region, assisted by a relative decline in both Thetford and Ipswich. It is likely that its status as a port was already threatened by Great Yarmouth in the twelfth century but the diversification of industrial, commercial and administrative importance in Norwich was sufficiently advanced that wealth would continue to accumulate. This, however, was secular wealth; Norwich was also exceptionally important as a Norman ecclesiastical centre, an aspect of its development which needs to be explored in the next chapter.

36 Articulated fish bones
(Mick Sharp)

4

NORMAN NORWICH –
THE ECCLESIASTICAL TOWN

The Normans almost certainly found Norwich to be a town of churches. It has been observed that a minimum of 25 were probably in existence by 1066 and that many of these churches were located on street corners of the Anglo-Scandinavian town. Some, such as St Clement Fybriggate and St Gregory, were clearly extensive in influence while others were held by great magnates, such as the Abbots of Ely and Bury or the Archbishop of Canterbury himself.

Norwich in 1066, however, was not the seat of the bishopric although the Bishop of East Anglia held land in the settlement including three-quarters of a mill, half an acre of meadow and a dwelling. The seat of the bishopric was at the rural site of Elmham; it was moved by Bishop Herfast about 1072 to Thetford in pursuit of final establishment at Bury St Edmunds. However, it is possible that the idea of settling the episcopal seat in Norwich was in some minds at least at the same time; William the Conqueror granted a block of property in Norwich to Herfast, a grant of about 1075 recorded as follows in Domesday Book: '14 dwellings which King William gave to E(rfast) for the principal seat of the Bishopric'. Herfast's claim to Bury was opposed by the abbot and the claim was abandoned in 1081 but the seat nevertheless remained in Thetford.

Herbert de Losinga, created bishop in 1090, determined to move the seat to Norwich and this was effected from 1094. Land was acquired in stages, building on the Conqueror's original grant with confirmation of 'the land of St Michael' sometime before 1100, the grant of the manor of Thorpe in 1101 (which included land west of the river, Thorpe itself lying to the east) and, in 1106, 'the land from the bishop's land to the water, and from the bridge of St Martin to the land of St Michael'. Together, these grants formed the area now occupied by the Cathedral Close plus land outside the Close which lay within the liberty of the bishopric.

Herbert was also empowered to augment the site of his episcopal seat with a Benedictine priory in a decree issued on Christmas Day 1100 by Henry I: 'in the church which is building … Herbert may place monks there who shall be irremovable'. The construction of the church seems to have started in 1096 and, like that of the castle, involved considerable destruction of the earlier Anglo-Saxon town. The destruction occurred after Domesday Book was compiled and thus is not recorded therein but it is clear that the churches of St Michael

76

Tombland and Holy Trinity were demolished and it is probable that entire streets of houses were also removed.

NORWICH CATHEDRAL

The cleared space was the site of a colossal building campaign. Construction of the great cathedral church (*colour plate 7*), where work started at the east end, was accompanied by the building of a palace for the bishop to the north and of monastic buildings for the priory to the south. In addition, a convent wall was built around the Close and gates were erected. The eastern end of the church, together with the transepts, tower and four bays of nave west of the tower, were completed by Herbert's death in 1119. His successor, Eborard, is said to have finished the church by the 1140s (*ecclesiam integraliter consummavit*) but the final consecration took place as late as 1278.

Despite alterations and depredations during the last 900 years, significant quantities of Norman work remain. The church itself is the greatest single survivor, with the nave, transepts, tower and presbytery being substantially Norman (except for the roofs and the clerestory of the presbytery). Although faced largely in Caen or Barnack limestone, the walls of the building are constructed in flint rubble with lime mortar. A section through the north wall of the north nave aisle was observed in 1988.

Unsurprisingly, archaeological excavation in and around the church has been limited other than for observations during remedial works and limited investigations at the west end and adjacent to the north transept. A major excavation was undertaken in 1930/31, however, by Dean Cranage, prior to the construction of a new chapel on the site of the destroyed Lady Chapel. This unearthed evidence for the original eastern apse of the building, complementing semicircular side chapels which survive, and confirming the plan of the cathedral as one based upon the Cluniac ideal of a church with an ambulatory around and behind the altar.

It is the plan of the cathedral which has inspired what is perhaps the most interesting archaeological detective work of recent years concerning the church and its associated buildings. While the orientation of the church is east-to-west (and possibly overlies directly the line of east-to-west Holme Street, the Roman road), analysis of the structure has convinced Professor Fernie that, mathematically, the layout of the building was conceived using the principle of one to the square root of two. This principle extended to a determination of the layout of the cloister and of the orientation of the bishop's palace.

A detailed survey of the church was undertaken in the 1790s by John Adey Repton whose magnificent drawings remained the best available until the 1990s. A new survey has now been completed by the University of Reading and this,

37 Filming for BBC Television of excavated apse beneath east end of cathedral church (Brian Ayers)

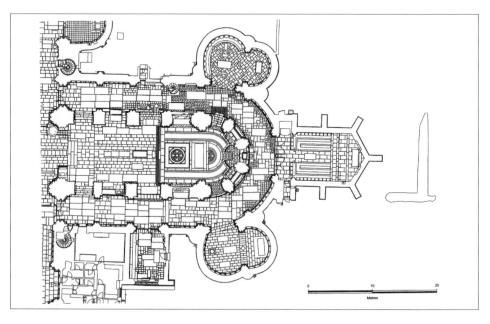

38 Survey drawing of the east end of the cathedral church (Roland B. Harris and Philip Thomas; by permission of the Chapter of Norwich Cathedral)

together with detailed observation of ongoing conservation work, is already enabling new discovery and assisting interpretation of the building. As examples, surprising survivals of original Romanesque stonework have been discovered on the exterior of the central tower while work on the north transept in 1996 has enabled a reconstruction of the Romanesque gable.

South and north of the church, both cloister and palace contain much original Norman work. The cloister was badly damaged in a riot of 1272 and its public face was rebuilt in perpendicular style, but internally much Norman blind arcading is visible as are the distinctive interior windows of the refectory to the south. West of the cloister was a guest wing (with so-called 'Saxon' basket windows) while the dormitory, reredorter and chapter house lay to the east. The refectory, which has been described as 'one of the most splendid in Europe' was unroofed in the eighteenth century when a canon's house and garden were constructed within it. These have now gone and the refectory has been transformed into a modern refectory for visitors to the cathedral. Limited excavations uncovered quantities of carved stone, floor tiles and an enigmatic stone feature located centrally against the south wall. This structure is tentatively interpreted as the base of a stair to the reading pulpit but its location is unparalleled in any other known Benedictine institution.

More extensive excavations in 2006 uncovered the remains of the guest wing or hostry. This had been terraced into the hillslope, removing most of the pre-Conquest deposits, but substantial elements of the lower walls of the building

39 Excavation of the site of the Hostry (© Roland B. Harris)

survived, including such details as a probable small *lavatorium* for the guests. This feature was set into the west face of the cloister wall, back-to-back with the extant monastic *lavatorium* in the west walk of the cloister and presumably sharing the same water supply and drain.

Further demolition included the chapter house off the east walk of the cloister, most of the dormitory range and the infirmary. Excavation in 1889 revealed an apsidal east end to the Romanesque chapter house while traces of the vaults to the dormitory undercroft have been recorded (and can still be seen) on the surviving elements of its eastern and western walls. The infirmary stood to the south of the refectory; it dated to about 1175 with a large nave and south aisle. Piers of the aisle remain as do parts of the south wall. This adjoined the infirmarer's hall and camera, parts of which survive within 63/65 The Close. Work here in 2000-01 recorded features such as part of a hall window and uncovered a length of the hitherto unknown Great Drain of the priory. This structure was built of flint and limestone rubble and consisted of side walls supporting a barrel vault 1.2m wide internally and some 2m high. It lies beneath late twelfth-century Caen stone arches which in turn support the monastic buildings above. Observations of commercial excavations elsewhere have made it possible to postulate a total length of some 500m for the priory's drainage system.

The bishop's palace was originally linked to the north aisle of the nave of the cathedral church but it was 'disjoined' in the 1850s. Although grievously converted to school use in 1958-9, substantial traces of Norman work survive, including a vaulted undercroft and, masked by later additions, what is essentially the earliest (and probably smallest) tower keep in Norfolk. Part of the earlier graveyard, postulated as that of the pre-Conquest church of Holy Trinity (above) runs beneath the palace footings.

The bishop and his prior stressed the links of the new church with the ancient seat of the bishopric by transferring the remains of the Saxon bishop's throne to a new site behind the high altar. The much-damaged fragments of this throne survive as does an effigy which was purpose-built for a niche above the exterior doorway to the north transept. This effigy, probably the earliest post-Roman large-scale figurative sculpture in England, was once thought to represent Bishop Herbert. It is now more generally felt to depict St Felix, who converted East Anglia to Christianity. Such a representation provided further emphasis of links with the past and legitimised the translation of the seat of the bishopric to its new location.

Links between the monastic precinct and the earlier town were provided by the continued existence of pre-Conquest churches within the Close. Not all were destroyed to clear the area and the churches of St Ethelbert, St Helen and St Mary-in-Marsh continued in use. St Helen was demolished about 1249 when the parish was amalgamated with the newly founded Great Hospital and St Ethelbert was destroyed in a riot of 1272 (geophysical survey undertaken in the

40 Interior of the north side of the
Ethelbert Gate (Brian Ayers)

1970s suggests that remains of the church lie beneath the lawn of Almary Green).
St Mary survived as a church into the sixteenth century with ruins standing 200
years later. These were incorporated into the Georgian terrace of Nos 10-12 The
Close, the north wall of the church providing the spine wall of the houses.

Most of the walls enclosing the cathedral precinct also survive and, while
much repair work has been undertaken, late eleventh-century and twelfth-
century elements clearly still stand. One such element can be observed within the
Ethelbert Gate, which leads out of the Close into the southern part of Tombland.
The original gate was destroyed in 1272 but its successor was created by reusing
much of the Norman gateway and walls. In consequence, parts of the precinct
wall of c.1100 can still be seen as can quoins which probably formed the jambs
of the interior gateway. These quoins retain distinctive Norman diagonal tooling,
as well as fire damage probably sustained in 1272.

Water access to the precinct was facilitated by the construction of a canal from
the river Wensum to the lower Close. Traditionally it is asserted that this was
effected to allow ease of transport for stone to the cathedral and tradition may
well be correct although presumably it also provided the bishop and the prior
with their own quay and thus they could avoid tolls. The canal could still be used
in the eighteenth century; a keel or wherry is depicted sailing up to the cathedral

in a prospect of the city drawn in the 1720s. However, the canal was referred to as a 'stinking ditch' by the mid-nineteenth century and was infilled.

The canal was well-placed to facilitate the movement of stone shipments reaching Norwich from the coast but it was also sited opposite stone quarries on the east bank of the river Wensum. These quarries, traces of which still exist, were located at the foot of a steep hill leading up on to Mousehold Heath and must have been exploited for the vast quantities of flint and lime which were needed. They were within the manor of Thorpe and thus on episcopal land, standing on either side of the Roman road from Brundall. Exploitation took a different form in later centuries; in 1771 Sylas Neville, waiting for a chaise outside the city gate, 'found three curious Fossils, worth at least 15 shillings'. This consoled him for the expense of the chaise!

The ecclesiastical manor of Thorpe also provided timber of which the cathedral and its associated buildings would have required great quantities. Bishop Herbert was aware of the precious nature of this resource and, about 1100, issued orders for effective conservation of Thorpe Wood. Resources for the cathedral priory were also drawn from further afield, sometimes with consequent impact upon the environment. Some 400,000 peat turves *per annum* were being burnt by the priory in the fourteenth century with similar quantities no doubt being required two centuries earlier. The turbaries from which they were extracted lay east of the city and eventually flooded to form the Norfolk Broads.

OTHER MONASTIC FOUNDATIONS

At the top of the steep hill to Mousehold Heath, on the southern side of the road, was another monastic institution, St Leonard's Priory. This was also founded by Bishop Herbert, reputedly before the foundation of the cathedral. It was served by monks from the cathedral and little now survives although there are fragmentary ruins amongst private gardens. The monks also served a small chapel to the north of the road. This was dedicated to St Michael and was built by Herbert in recompense for his destruction of the important pre-Conquest church of St Michael on Tombland. Most of this has been destroyed as well although a large section of the north wall still stands, constructed in courses of well-sorted flint cobbles.

Herbert de Losinga was clearly an energetic man for, not content with the cathedral precinct, St Leonard's Priory, St Michael's Chapel and new churches in both Lynn and Yarmouth, he also founded two hospitals. One of these was dedicated to St Mary Magdalen and it stood to the north of the city on what is now Sprowston Road. This hospital, which became known as the Lazar House because of its association with lepers (although it does not seem to have been exclusively for their use), was furnished with its own graveyard and chapel. Burials from the graveyard were recorded during construction works of the adjacent Gilman Road, some of them exhibiting leprosy in the bone. The infirmary hall survives, converted to a public library. It has two decorated doorways and may originally have had a third.

The other foundation of Bishop Herbert seems to have been that of St Paul's or Norman's Hospital. This stood to the north of the river (within the city), linked to the south bank and to the Close by a bridge, that of St Martin. It occupied land which was part of the episcopal manor of Thorpe and therefore came within the liberty of the cathedral rather than that of the city. The area was lowlying and was probably situated immediately east of the eastern arm of the Anglo-Scandinavian defences. Here the second bishop, Eborard, completed the hospital which was linked with the parochial church of St Paul. Although it occupied a large area, and was endowed generously by patrons (including the king), nothing now remains. It is possible that a later medieval wall uncovered in excavations at the eastern perimeter of the site in 1992 may represent part of its precinct wall. St Paul's church has also been destroyed, in its case by enemy action in 1942.

THE PRIOR'S FEE

The lands acquired by the bishop, on both banks of the river, passed into the control of the prior with the prior's fee being exempt, like the castle, from city dues and taxation. The rights and privileges of the prior were to cause problems with the citizens for centuries, only being resolved as late as 1524 following intervention by Cardinal Wolsey. Investigation of the prior's fee continues to cause problems to the present day.

Primarily this is due to a lack of opportunity for archaeological work. The largest single area is that of the cathedral precinct and this is generally free of development pressure. As has been seen, archaeological work is therefore largely confined to small-scale excavation or watching brief work. It is correspondingly difficult to chart the development of the Close through the buried archaeological record although significant strides have been made with architectural and archaeological analysis of standing buildings. The recent work at the infirmarer's hall suggests strongly that there may be even more Norman work surviving within parts of the Close than is generally realised. In particular it is likely that the granary vaults date from the twelfth century as does part of the building on the site of the prior's boathouse.

Outside the Close, some archaeological work has been undertaken on the Fee. It was noted above (p.71) that excavation and documentary research at St Martin-at-Palace Plain indicated that the area was laid out afresh in the twelfth century, almost certainly as a result of ecclesiastical intervention. The excavated stone building paid rents to the cellarer of the cathedral and it is also known that the cellarer took rents from a further stone house immediately outside the Ethelbert Gate on Tombland. The area of St Paul's church and hospital, however, together with the 17 or so houses known to have been built nearby, remains largely unexplored.

CHURCHES

The church of St Paul indicates that church foundation did not stop with the Norman Conquest. Indeed it seems likely that the great market church of St Peter Mancroft was founded before 1075 and was probably the church held by the priest Wala in 1086. This was a foundation by a lay lord, Earl Ralph de Guader, and in this it seems to have continued a pre-Conquest tradition of the establishment of churches as proprietary churches or *Eigenkirchen* by individuals. Similarly the church of St Giles was reputedly founded in the Conqueror's reign by Elwyn the priest on his own estate.

Other churches probably established in the late eleventh or early twelfth century include St George Colegate and St George Tombland. St George, a popular dedication after the First Crusade of 1096, was probably given to a new church on Colegate as occupation expanded westward along the north bank of the river in the twelfth century, linking the (once-fortified) area around Magdalen Street with the early nucleus of occupation at the southern end of Oak Street. St George Tombland appears to be an encroachment on Tombland, the site of the pre-Conquest market place but one where commercial importance had been eclipsed by the establishment of a new market area in the Norman borough. Construction of St George also seems to have blocked partially the alignment of the east-to-west Roman road (much of which had already been destroyed by the building of the cathedral), necessitating a bend in the line of Princes Street and, possibly, also leading to the establishment of the right-of-way through the churchyard which acts as a 'remembrance' of the lost road. Excavation north of the church behind the Samson and Hercules building in 2007 located burials probably associated with an overly ambitious churchyard which was soon reduced in size, together with a suggestion of the earlier market frontage.

It is possible to reconstruct other probable topographical details from the position of St George Colegate or, rather, its parish boundary. St George seems to have been carved out of the earlier large parish of St Clement and the boundary between the two parishes south of Colegate runs directly towards the river before veering eastwards. This is paralleled to the west by the line of Water Lane which also runs directly south from Colegate before veering westwards. The effect is one of a funnel on the north bank of the river Wensum and it has been suggested that the boundary and lane may mark the edges of the original outflow of the Muspole stream.

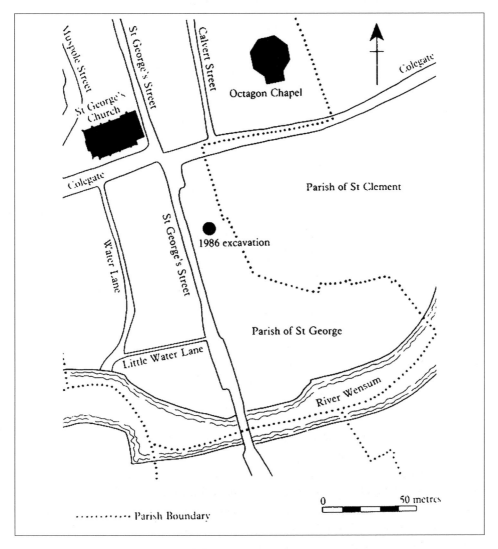

41 Map showing Water Lane and the boundary between the parishes of St Clement and St George (Jayne Bown)

This hypothesis was tested by a very small excavation in 1986 behind buildings on St George's Street (which now links Colegate to the river between the parish boundary and Water Lane). The work discovered deep deposits of infilled material at a point 94m north of the river, suggesting that the hypothesis may be correct. The infilling itself could date from the twelfth century as a further church, St Margaret Newbridge, is known to have stood off St George's Street near the river by 1157. The 'new bridge' itself is recorded by 1257 although this too could be a Norman innovation. After 1359 the church was converted to a hermitage chapel with the hermit having charge of the bridge.

Another church dedicated to St Margaret was that of St Margaret *in combusto* at the northern end of Magdalen Street. Although this church ceased to function in the fifteenth century, and was probably demolished by the sixteenth century, the site has been excavated (partially in 1973 and again in 1987). Remains of the building had been comprehensively destroyed by the cellars of a nineteenth-century Blind Institute but a large part of the graveyard was uncovered. This came into use about 1100 and clearly served an impoverished parish.

No memorials were discovered at St Margaret and these are indeed uncommon until late in the Middle Ages. A memorial stone of twelfth-century date was re-used in the construction of the medieval city wall, however, near the King Street gate. It was recovered in 1924 and has a Latin inscription seeking prayers for the soul of Bertrand de Fun...eki (the name is partly indecipherable). It is not known which

42 Excavation of bombed church of St Benedict (Norwich Survey)

graveyard it came from although the nearest would have been that of St Peter Southgate, a church probably in existence by the last quarter of the twelfth century.

Partial excavation has also been undertaken in another Norman church, that of St James. The earliest documentary reference to this parish is 1180. Limited work during conversion of the church building to a puppet theatre in 1979 revealed that the earliest phase of the structure consisted of an aisleless nave with a long narrow chancel built of roughly knapped flint. A number of fragments of twelfth-century architectural detailing were also recovered, including sections of Romanesque colonnette shafts and voussoir blocks with diamond lozenges and spiked foliate decoration. The stone is Caen, suggesting a possible link with the cathedral priory although the bishop did not take control of the living until 1201. The church stood, however, on episcopal land with a parish which extended out of the growing city into the surrounding areas of Pockthorpe and Mousehold Heath (also episcopal land).

Other churches can be suggested as Norman foundations such as St Michael-at-Thorn (destroyed by bombing in 1942), St Julian (also bombed but rebuilt) and possibly St Benedict (bombed in 1942 and excavated in the 1970s). The site of St Michael is now used as a surface car park but it would clearly repay excavation should development take place, especially as it had a Norman doorway. This was salvaged after the Second World War and transferred to the rebuilt St Julian. Here, the round tower and 'basket' windows are often taken to indicate pre-Conquest origin but the foundation could date as easily to the late eleventh or early twelfth century.

TWELFTH-CENTURY FOUNDATIONS

A further Norman creation was that of St William's chapel upon Mousehold Heath to the east of the city. The boy William was murdered in 1144, was canonised subsequently and a shrine established in the cathedral. The site of the discovery of his body was marked by the construction of a chapel, earthworks of which remain.

The greatest Norman church of Norwich after the cathedral, however, was that of the priory at Carrow (immediately south of the city). This was founded about 1146 as a Benedictine nunnery and grew rapidly to become one of the largest and most important such houses in the country. Ruins still stand, notably of the cloister and the prioress's lodging, but also of the dormitory undercroft, the chapter house, slype and the church itself.

Excavations prior to consolidation in 1981 revealed remains of tiled floors dating from the twelfth to the fifteenth centuries and nine graves of adult females. The plan as visible was largely excavated in 1881. The church was 60m (195ft)

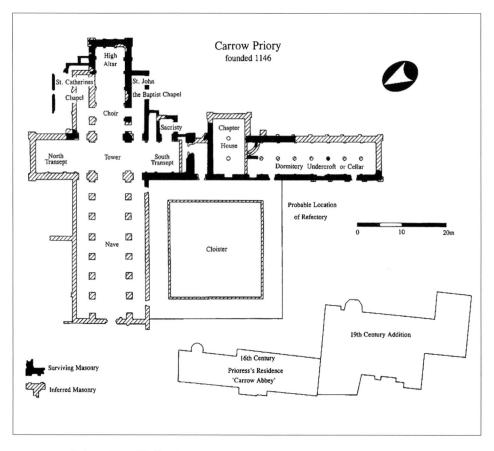

43 Carrow Priory (Piers Wallace)

in length with a rectangular chancel and transepts with chapels. A complete thirteenth-century jar recovered in 1968 (with an inscription apparently *ADAM*) may have been used as an acoustic jar in one of the priory walls. The priory stood on a low rise between the Wensum and Yare valleys and must have dominated the confluence of these two rivers and the downstream approach to Norwich.

The Norman legacy to Norwich, therefore, is very great. Ecclesiastical foundations and secular institutions, together with a major expansion of the area of settlement, produced a city of the first rank by the end of the twelfth century. It is a city where archaeological exploration, both above and below ground, continues to reveal evidence of Norman activity. Norwich received its first charter in the reign of Henry II but it was the 1194 charter of Richard I, at the end of the Norman period, which characterises best the emerging nature of the settlement. This enabled the citizens to elect their own reeve instead of being governed by a royal official. Norwich was ceasing to be a mere borough and was emerging as a great medieval city.

5

NORWICH
BEFORE THE BLACK DEATH

It is possible to reconstruct a map of Norwich on the eve of the Black Death (1349) which depicts a city of extraordinary size and complexity. An urban area some 1.5 miles from north-to-south and one mile from east-to-west, bounded by a defensive wall and ditch on three sides, stands on both banks of the river Wensum which is itself crossed by no fewer than five bridges. Within the defended area is a royal castle, a Benedictine monastery and cathedral, four large friary precincts, several hospitals, nearly 70 parish churches, a commercial waterfront, warehouses, markets, houses of an affluent merchant class and homes of the urban poor. The city is larger in area than London and Southwark combined and, although its population is inferior to that of London, at about 30,000, is still exceptional for the Middle Ages.

This great city was a product of the development described in the foregoing chapters. The consolidation of this development – building upon the city's role as a market, an industrial centre, a port and an administrative centre (both secular and ecclesiastical) – was essentially a phenomenon of the thirteenth century. It is at this period that it is possible to view the city emerging as a cohesive unit, with citizens who were consciously seeking to extend the liberties of Norwich.

CITY WALLS

The most tangible reminder of this idea, that of promoting the city as its own entity, survives today in the ruins of the city wall. Work started on a communal defensive system, which also defined the city and allowed control of trade, in 1253. A bank was erected with upcast material from a ditch and, presumably, a timber revetment was set on top of the bank. The ditch cut through the prior's land at Pockthorpe on the north bank of the river, an assertion of the citizens' power which raised strong objection from the ecclesiastical authorities.

The first murage grant, enabling a masonry wall to be built, was made in 1297. The complete circuit was not finished until 1344 and, even then, was only achieved when a wealthy private citizen, Richard Spynk, paid for considerable stretches out of his own purse. There were over 40 towers and 12 gates, using

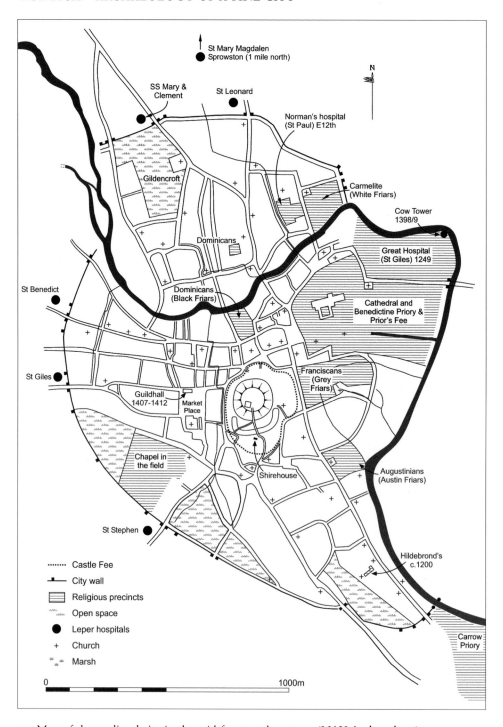

44 Map of the medieval city in the mid-fourteenth century (NAU Archaeology)

45 Interior of the King Street gate in the eighteenth century (Norfolk Museums & Archaeology Service)

prodigious quantities of flint and mortar. Boom towers were erected at the southern end where the wall met the river, enabling a chain of Spanish iron to be stretched across the Wensum to inhibit river traffic.

The gates were all pulled down between 1791 and 1810 although it is possible to gain an impression of them from a series of eighteenth-century engravings. The south side of St Benedict's Gate survived until 1942, complete with a door-pin, but this ruin was destroyed in the 'Baedeker' air raid of April that year. None of the gates has been excavated although foundations of St Stephen's Gate, the main gate to London and Ipswich, were uncovered during the construction of underpasses for the Inner Ring Road in 1964. A sketch plan is the only known record.

More recently, in 1998, the south wall of the gate tower above Bishop Bridge was exposed when post-medieval infilling material was removed to allow access to a viewing point on the river. The revealed wall can now be seen and is constructed of well-dressed limestone. Detailed analysis of the stonework which is chamfered towards the river, combined with eighteenth-century drawings of the tower before its demolition, not only enabled a reconstruction drawing but also the provision of a virtual reality 'fly-through' impression of the building. The gateway was one of the elements of the defences paid for by Spynk; the outer arch of the bridge beneath has a string-course decorated with a male and a female carved head, possibly representations of Spynk and his wife.

The walls and towers of the city wall have suffered grievously but considerable stretches still stand. Excavation has been limited save for work on Barn Road in

46 Excavation and survey
at Bishop Bridge 1998 (NAU
Archaeology)

47 City Wall at Chapelfield
Road (Brian Ayers)

1948 and 1954 which uncovered the early bank, a ditch that was 4m (12ft) deep, 20m (60ft) wide and wet at this location, and a semi-circular projecting turret, trenches on Queen's Road in 1962/3 which revealed traces of an upcast gravel bank, and minor excavations north of the Wensum in 1987and 2008 at River Lane. The 1987 work uncovered the foundations of the wall, in an area where it approaches the river, and the threshold and door jamb of the turret which stood next to the river. These details were fashioned in brick although the wall and turret themselves were built of flint. The River Lane stretch appears to be a late addition to the circuit, possibly of *c*.1377.

The city wall was built in courses of flint which, because of the large quantities of mortar necessary, had to be erected in 'lifts', each lift of between 0.3m (1ft) and 0.5m (20in) in height being shuttered and allowed to set before the next 'lift' was added. It is often possible to detect such 'lifts' in the surviving stretches of wall. The full height of the wall was some 4m (12ft), the only surviving part at this height being next to the site of the Ber Street Gate where (much-restored) battlements can be seen finished in brick.

The exterior face of the wall was frequently built in front of an arcade which supported the wall-walk. This arcade survives in several places with the recesses within the arcade acting as embrasures for the arrow loops. The Carrow Hill section provides a good example. At Barn Road, the face of the wall has been removed but the arcade stands as a series of arches.

The wall-walk passed through the interval towers, doorways being extant at the Black Tower on Carrow Hill and on the tower next to the site of St Stephen's

48 Gunloop – Baker Lane (Brian Ayers)

Gate. This tower retains part of its brick vault above which the wall-walk passes. It also has the remains of two gun-loops for primitive artillery, probably amongst the earliest such loops in the country. A smaller loop, for a hand gun, survives in the stretch of wall between this tower and the gate. Other loops are known elsewhere, notably at Baker Lane where a particularly fine example is extant, fashioned in limestone rather than brick.

Parts of the circuit were served by lanes immediately inside the wall, providing ease of access. St Martin-at-Oak Wall Lane, Wellington Lane and Bull Lane are surviving examples. A short stretch of the now-lost intramural lane within the Chapelfield Raod stretch of the city wall was recorded in evaluation excavations undertaken in 2000.

The exceptionally large circuit of the defences encompassed most of the existing built-up area in the fourteenth century, although it excluded the hamlet of Heigham which thereafter developed as a small western suburb. The great sweep of wall necessitated the enclosure of open spaces as well, in order to reduce awkward salients, and some of these to the north and west remained open space into the eighteenth and nineteenth centuries (such as Gildencroft, twelve acres of land inside the north-western stretch of the walls which included a 'Justing Acre'). The defended area also included the commercial waterfront on King Street which seems to have been thriving by the thirteenth century. The southern end of the street in particular was busy: references are made to St Julian's Staith in 1275, Frankestathe in 1290 and St Olave's Staith in 1346.

WATERFRONT

Excavation on this waterfront itself has been restricted to date. Such work as has been possible, however, is encouraging. Small-scale excavation at Cannon Wharf revealed early timber revetments of willow and oak, demonstrating that preservation was good. Larger excavations further north behind Dragon Hall on King Street were set back from the immediate vicinity of the riverside but nevertheless uncovered a lane connecting the street to the river, late twelfth- or thirteenth-century timber buildings either side of this lane, one of which is interpreted as a warehouse and which burnt down, later thirteenth-century stone buildings, consistent evidence for the importation of fish and probable smoking of fish suggested by peat-fired hearths

Riverside activity continued upstream as well. Rushworth's Staith is recorded in 1291, probably near the outflow of the Dallingfleet stream into the river Wensum immediately south of the Cathedral Close. Much riverside shipment here must have been associated with the cathedral priory, not least supplying it with the hundreds of thousands of peat turves mentioned above which it burnt for fuel each year.

North of the Close, however, it is likely that wharfage facilities were reserved for small fishing craft or boats serving riverside industries. St Edmund's Quay off Fishergate may well have been used by fishermen in the twelfth and thirteenth centuries (a large anchor was reputedly found during the digging of a cellar in the parish of St Edmund in 1686) although the available documentation would suggest that, by the early fourteenth century, the river frontage had largely been taken over by skinners, tanners, fullers and dyers.

Fishing was important, nevertheless: herring pies were tendered to the Crown in the thirteenth century and had probably been offered earlier. Many fishermen were concentrated in the parish of St George Tombland, close to the cathedral, where a fish house is recorded in 1272. Another fish house is mentioned on Quayside in 1286; this belonged to Maud or Matilda of Catton who had blocked Quayside when she had it built. Shellfish were landed further west on Quayside. Rapid salvage excavation in 1963 beneath the site of the New Star Inn uncovered a layer of oyster shells 0.46m (18in) thick.

TRADE AND INDUSTRY

The gradual colonisation of the river foreshore by industry is particularly notable from the thirteenth century. Analysis of documents, especially the Enrolled Deeds (of 1285-1311 with later examples) has enabled a broad understanding of the disposition of craft industries throughout the city. This is particularly true of clothworkers such as dyers. These seem to have occupied the foreshore throughout the central part of the city although there was a distinct grouping of such workers in the Westwick Street area. The eastern part of Westwick Street was called Letestere Row (that is, Listers' or Dyers' Row) and it led to the Maddermarket where dyestuffs were sold (woad was imported from Amiens and Corbie after 1286). Two-thirds of the dyers mentioned in the Enrolled Deeds seem to have worked in this area.

Fullers were also cloth finishers who needed access to water and they were located close to the main group of dyers. All ten fullers in the Enrolled Deeds were mentioned in the western part of the city where also was 'Le Fulleres holes', a lane running to the river downstream of the dyers. Fullers needed clean water and it is difficult to see how this could be provided at Fullers Hole. A little further east was 'Bleckstershole', recorded from 1292, where the bleachers of woollen cloth worked. They also needed water and thus, with their colleagues the dyers and fullers, formed a considerable area of cloth finishing. They were joined by shearmen, who trimmed the nap on the cloth, and who occupied Shearing or Charing Cross between Letestere Row, Fullers Hole, Bleckstershole and the Maddermarket.

Although the cloth finishing trade was clearly important, the largest single industrial group in the city seems to have been that of the leatherworkers. These

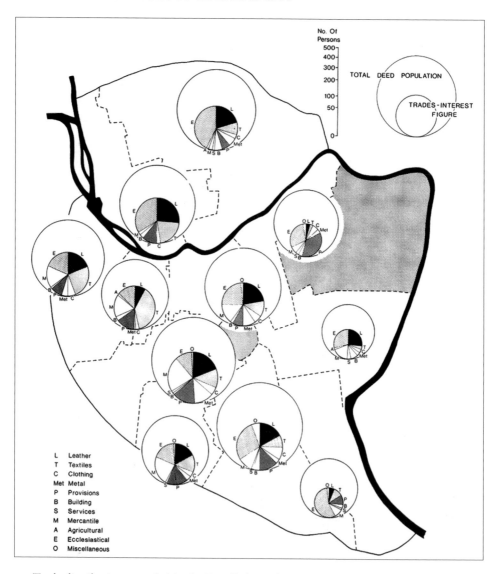

No. Of
Persons
500
400
300
200
100
50
0

TOTAL DEED POPULATION

TRADES-INTEREST
FIGURE

L   Leather
T   Textiles
C   Clothing
Met Metal
P   Provisions
B   Building
S   Services
M   Mercantile
A   Agricultural
E   Ecclesiastical
O   Miscellaneous

49 Trade distribution recorded in the Enrolled Deeds (Norwich Survey)

comprised skinners, tanners, tawyers, whitawyers, shoemakers, saddlers and parchment makers. The skinners, tanners and tawyers were most active next to the Wensum, in Conesford off Mountergate and next to the Muspole and Dalymond streams on the north bank of the river. Leatherdressers were grouped in St Giles parish although cordwainers or workers in fine leather were largely centred on the Market Place.

Textile and leather workers were not the only trades-people at the waterfront. Excavation off King Street at Dragon Hall has uncovered a probable fish-house where herring was smoked, the first such to be found in Norwich.

Right: 1 Excavation at Dragon Hall, King Street (Jason Dawson/NAU Archaeology)

Below: 2 Excavation of prehistoric ring-ditch and a seventh-century Saxon cemetery at Harford Farm, Norwich Southern Bypass 1989 (Derek A. Edwards, © Norfolk Museums & Archaeology Service)

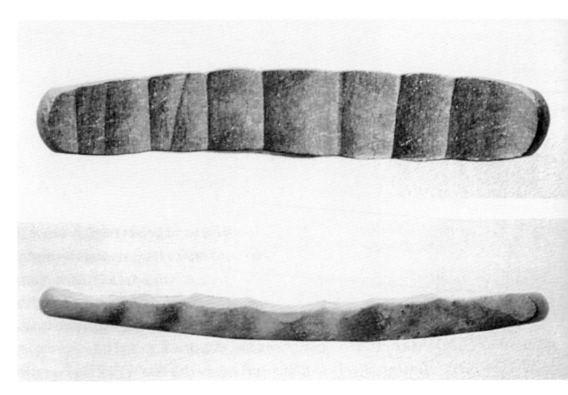

3 Gold Viking Age ingot from the Forum site 1999 (NAU Archaeology)

4 Cathedral hostry excavation – coin of Cnut (David Dobson/NAU Archaeology)

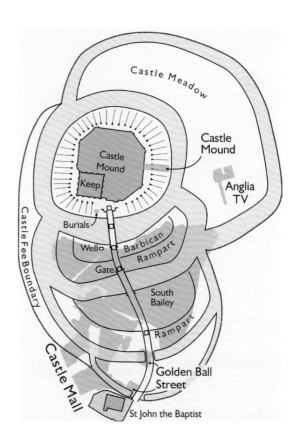

5 Schematic plan showing the castle earthworks following remodelling in the thirteenth century (David Dobson, NAU Archaeology)

6 Castle Mall excavation 1989 (Derek A. Edwards, © Norfolk Museums & Archaeology Service)

Above: 7 Norwich Cathedral (Brian Ayers)

Left: 8 Medieval road excavated beneath the Franciscan friary, 1991 (Phil Emery/NAU Archaeology)

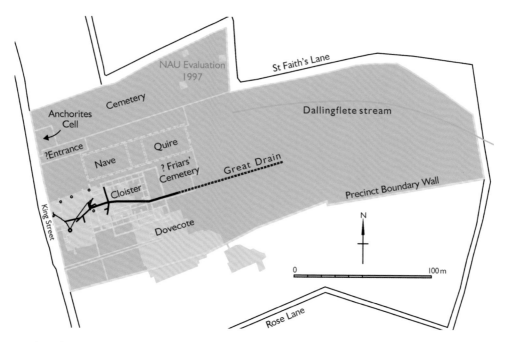

9 Plan of the Franciscan friary precinct around 1300 based upon evidence from excavations (in blue) and fifteenth- and sixteenth-century records (David Dobson, NAU Archaeology)

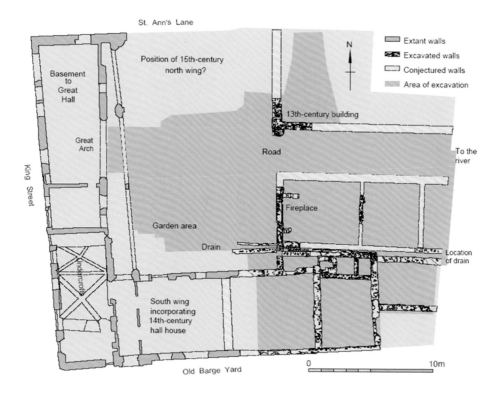

10 Plan of the Dragon Hall complex showing the undercrofts and the ground-floor basement to the hall connected to the river by an arch and a road (David Dobson, NAU Archaeology)

Left: 11 Excavating a limekiln at the Forum site 1999 (Jason Dawson/NAU Archaeology)

Below: 12 Oyster shell from the Franciscan friary which has been used as a painter's palette. Traces of vermilion (red), azurite (blue) & calcium carbonate (white) survive (NAU Archaeology)

13 Late fourteenth- or early fifteenth-century brooch from within a malting oven at the Forum site (Jason Dawson/NAU Archaeology)

14 Excavation of a skeleton in a stone sarcophagus at the cathedral hostry in 2006 (David Adams/ NAU Archaeology)

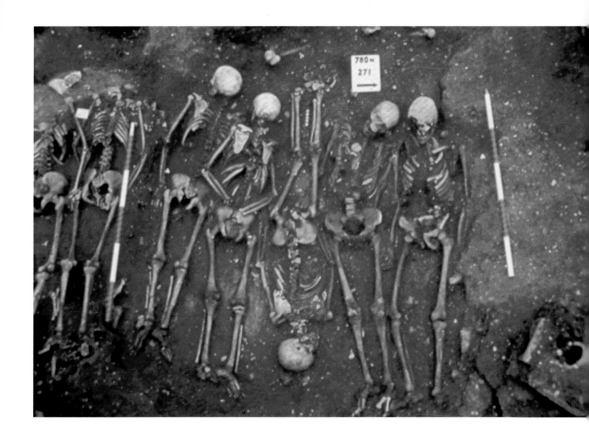

Above: 15 Excavation of burials
– some executed criminals buried
prone – at the site of St Margaret in
combusto, Magdalen Street in 1987
(Kirk Laws-Chapman)

Left: 16 Cow Tower, an artillery
fortification of 1398-99 (Brian Ayers)

17 Papal bulla or seal of Boniface VIII (1294-1303) from Palace Street. The seal would have been attached to a document and shows the heads of SS Paul (left) and Peter (David Adams/NAU Archaeology)

18 Heraldic glass from the Carmelite friary (Oxford Archaeology East)

19 Decorative boss in Norwich Cathedral cloisters (Brian Ayers)

20 Thorp Chapel at St Michael Coslany of about 1500 (Brian Ayers)

Right: 21 Interior of fifteenth-century rebuild of St Peter Mancroft (Brian Ayers)

Below: 22 East front of the Guildhall (Brian Ayers)

Left: 23 Fifteenth-century Norwich School painted glass in the Guildhall (Brian Ayers)

Below: 24 Conservation of wall painting in St Gregory (NAU Archaeology)

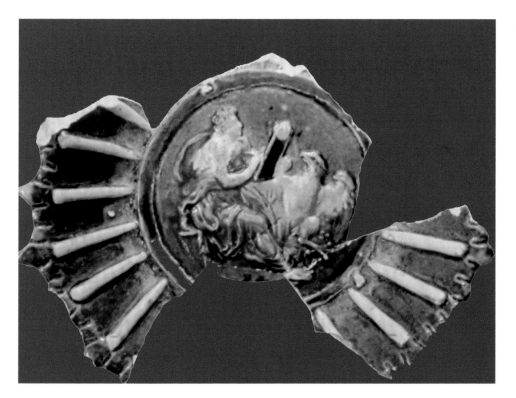

25 Sixteenth-century south-west French Palissy Ware dish depicting St John the evangelist from Castle Mall excavation (NAU Archaeology)

26 Elm Hill, rebuilt after fire of 1507 (Brian Ayers)

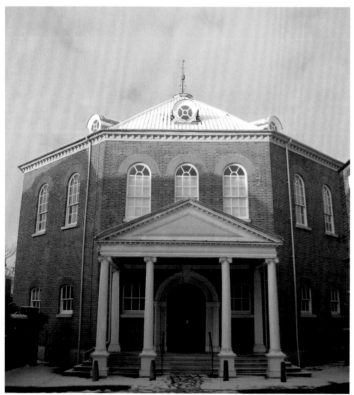

Above: 27 The probable Goldsmiths Hall of about 1700, dominating the public display space in front of the Guildhall (Brian Ayers)

Left: 28 Thomas Ivory's Octagon Chapel of 1756 (Brian Ayers)

29 Teacup from Anabaptist burial (Oxford Archaeology East)

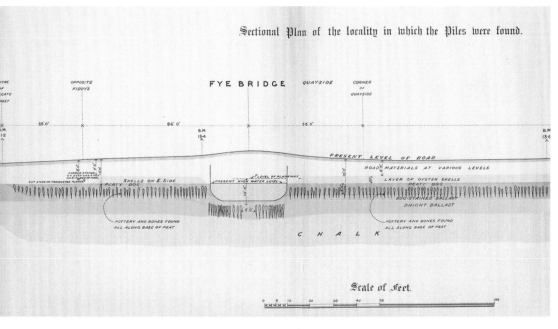

30 Section drawn of pre-Conquest causeway at Fye Bridge in 1896 (Norfolk & Norwich Archaeological Society)

Above: 31 Interior of Marble Hall of 1903-4 Norwich Union building (Norwich HEART)

Left: 32 New build at the river Wensum 2007 (Brian Ayers)

50 Fragment of fourteenth-century mould for casting a large, openwork Annunciation pilgrim badge found at Cinema City, St Andrew's Hall Plain (NAU Archaeology)

Increased colonisation of the river foreshore, and the larger numbers of people living on both banks of the river, probably necessitated the construction of a further bridge, New Bridge, by 1257. This, with Bishop Bridge (constructed originally about 1250 and re-built and fortified by Richard Spynk in the fourteenth century) brought to five the number of bridges across the river in the city centre, greatly in excess of bridge provision in any other medieval English city.

The riverside industries were complemented by other industries throughout the city. The Enrolled Deeds also mention goldsmiths, smiths, cutlers, lorimers (harness makers), latoners (brass workers), bell-founders, tailors, glovers, hatters, hosiers, girdlers, masons, carpenters, painters, roofers, coopers and boatmen among a total of some 68 different trades and services. Archaeological evidence for the products of these industries can be seen in the knives and padlocks recovered from excavations, in the remains of barrels often reused to line pits, in the recovery of a mould for manufacturing pilgrim badges or in the walls of surviving thirteenth- and fourteenth-century structures (notably the defences). Mercantile activity is hinted at by an incomplete balance pan from the Dragon Hall site. Not everything took place within the city walls; evidence for crop processing and hornworking was recovered from the suburb of Barrack Street in 2000.

Locally-produced goods were supplemented by imports, and documents and archaeological excavation combine to illustrate the range of Norwich's trade contacts. Building stone came from France, material from Caen being transhipped in Yarmouth in 1288/9. Wine was brought from the Rhineland and, occasionally, from Gascony (sherds of Saintonge pottery, rare in Norwich, were found at the Magistrates' Courts site in 1981 and in the Greyfriars' precinct in 1993). Steel was imported from Sweden and silks from Italy. Everyday pottery was also imported; the city was served with the products of east Norfolk kilns as well as the major west Norfolk industry centred on Pott Row, Grimston. Vast quantities of these types, as well as more exotic vessels, are located on excavations.

The diversity of goods available for sale, as well as the range of services which a great urban centre needed to provide, ensured that the market system was equally diverse. By the thirteenth century there were specialist markets at All Saints Green (swine, replaced by timber), Orford Hill (swine), Rampant Horse Street (horses – *Forum Equorum* in the reign of Edward I) and White Lion Street (saddlers). The Maddermarket has already been mentioned and to this can perhaps be added Wensum Street (*Vicus Cocorum* or Cookrow).

The Market Place itself, originally laid out in the eleventh century, had the greatest range of goods for sale. Poultry, sheep, cattle, wheat, wood and cheese were sold to the south of St Peter Mancroft church. To the north were drapers, linendrapers, clothiers, glovers, spicers, ironmongers, shoemakers, butchers, fishermen, cutlers, hatters and goldsmiths. There was even an apothecary market (*Forum Unguentor*). Tolls and customs were collected in the Murage Loft.

The survival of works of art implies that the city acted as a centre for specialised activities. It is likely that the writing and decoration of books was practised in Norwich and the Ormesby Psalter, now in the Bodleian Library, Oxford, is probably an example of such local output. Decorative ironworking, some as early as 1180 surviving on the doors of the cathedral infirmary, was probably also a local craft, with further examples on the doors of the Carnary College at the cathedral dating from about 1316-37. More mundane structural ironwork such as hinge pivots (one was found *in situ* on the twelfth-century building at the Magistrates' Courts site), hinges (a thirteenth or fourteenth-century example was recovered from Westwick Street) and keys would all have been made locally.

Sculpture was probably also practised in Norwich; all the large-scale sculpture of the medieval city has been destroyed (the last, of Christ displaying his wounds from the Ethelbert Gate, as late as 1964) but the wealth of small sculpture, such as that on the exquisite Prior's Door at the cathedral of about 1310, suggests a significant school. A stone carver called 'Guillaume de Nourriche' worked in Paris between 1297 and 1330 and may have been an expatriate product of such a school; an apostle by him is in the Musée de Cluny. A fine assemblage of thirteenth-century glass was recovered from excavations in the cathedral refectory in 2001, possibly another local product.

POPULATION AND HOUSING

The range of goods and services available in Norwich implies a large population, a conclusion endorsed by the apparent continued growth in the number of churches. Excluding religious houses, nearly 60 parish churches are known to have existed in the thirteenth century with very few going out of use. St Christopher seems to have burnt down before 1286 and was not rebuilt; St Edward was united with St Julian before 1300; and St John the Evangelist was pulled down about 1300. Development for insurance offices on the site of St John in 1964 removed much of the graveyard of this church.

This large number of churches, assuming a minimum congregation of some 250 souls to a church, implies a population of at least 15,000 people in the city. Recent analysis of the Mancroft Tithing Roll, however, would suggest that this could be a considerable underestimate. Extrapolation from the Mancroft sample indicates that a more realistic assessment would be a population well in excess of 20,000 and possibly as high as 30,000. Such numbers in the Middle Ages implied a great city indeed and it is small wonder that Norwich was a complex organisation, tied together by its bridges and churches and surrounded by its extensive city wall.

Excavation is beginning to provide considerable information on the lives of this medieval population. Housing, for example, is an area where little survives above ground to indicate the conditions within which people existed. It is becoming clear that the majority of people in the thirteenth and early fourteenth centuries occupied either timber-built structures or buildings with clay walls. These houses were usually single-storied and frequently had only one room. A central hearth was often, but not always, provided.

Examples of clay-walled buildings have been located at Alms Lane, Bishopgate, Botolph Street and, outside the city wall, on Heigham Street. Documentary evidence mentions such structures as in 1287 when Richard, son of William Pikot, and Matilda his wife granted a piece of land in Lower Newport (St Giles Street) to John le Lung, chaplain, and undertook 'that a wall of earth shall be built at the joint expense of the parties'. Occasionally there is evidence of clay and stone being used together, as at Westwick Street where excavation in 1972 demonstrated that the long walls of a building were supported by stone but the gable walls were of clay. Thatch was probably the most common roofing material but the recovery of an oak shingle at St Martin-at-Palace Plain in 1981 (complete with iron nail for attachment) demonstrated that wooden tiles were used too.

Post-built or clay buildings seem therefore to have been the norm for the mass of the population. Excavation also has the greatest potential as the primary source for information about buildings of greater social status at this period as well. No building belonging to the merchant class survives from the thirteenth century, although it can be surmised that many such structures would have been built with rubble ground-floor walls and timber-framing above (as was probably the case on the site of Dragon Hall, King Street). An example of such a structure was recorded on the 1975 Botolph Street site where a building complex comprised a two storey block of flint rubble behind a probable timber hall. A largely stone hall of fourteenth-century date was excavated at the Ben Burgess site on King Street in 1999. Here the hall stood at right-angles to the street with a service range running the width of the property.

The large population of Norwich was thus probably housed in generally poor conditions. The number of people would also have produced great quantities of rubbish material. Much of this was inevitably disposed of in rear tenement yards. Some houses had cesspits attached as in the example at the Ben Burgess site but pits in rear yards were also used; a barrel at Fishergate (excavated in 1985) contained human faecal residues dating from the fourteenth century. In addition there was presumably some nightsoil manuring of the fields around the city. There seems also to have been a trade in muck; the Great Plumstead estate paid for muck to be brought from Norwich in both 1277/8 and 1298/9. The trade was probably long-lasting as the muck boat was repaired in 1319/20.

It would appear that significant quantities of rubbish were also dumped at the river margins, not only to level up wharfage sites but also to remove low-lying land from danger of inundation. This would explain, for instance, the extensive deposits of rubbish material, mixed with occasional flood deposits, located off Whitefriars on the north bank of the river. Other sites also received rubbish; *Lothmere*, the name meaning 'muddy pool' was located off St Giles and is documented in use as a rubbish pit in 1289.

Floods were a considerable problem in the thirteenth-century city. A particularly bad flood is recorded in 1290 by Bartholomew Cotton which 'overturned some houses and bore them along'. A freshwater flood deposit was discovered within the stone building excavated at Palace Plain in 1981. Attempts were made to prevent flood incursions; the threshold of the north doorway of the stone building, which faced the river, was raised and the lower part of the doorway blocked by inserted flintwork.

The increasing numbers of people, and thereby houses, in the thirteenth century meant that much of the tenement pattern of the medieval city was established at this time with boundaries either being created afresh or being established through subdivision of existing plots. At Calvert Street, on the north bank of the river, a boundary between two properties was marked initially by a wooden fence, the large post-holes for which were clearly visible. These respected the position of the now anachronistic Anglo-Scandinavian defensive bank, implying that the boundary was established by the twelfth century at the latest. It was succeeded by a flint wall with this, in turn, being replaced by a brick wall and the boundary again surviving until recent times. South of the river, at Dragon Hall, properties were re-aligned and, although the internal boundaries were lost in the fifteenth century, the thirteenth-century layout determined the form of the building which survives today, decisions made over 700 years ago still influencing the modern topography.

This development of the urban geographic pattern was one which also removed existing streets where these were no longer used to great effect. In 1250 Roger de Burg was fined for obstructing the King's way upon the quay (at the eastern end of Quayside) and was ordered to clear his purpresture or encroachment. He may have done so but in 1285/6 four further defendants – including Maud de Catton – were all accused of blocking the quay and of having 'built Houses there to the nuisance of ye whole City & of all Passengers and Boats there arriving ...'. These houses may have remained, despite orders for their demolition, for the line of Quayside is blocked on the earliest detailed map of the city (1558) and remains blocked to this day.

The people who lived and died in the city were generally buried in the local cemeteries around the parish churches. While some 30 parish churches survive, another 30 or so have been lost (many in the sixteenth century). It is inevitable that redevelopment will affect such sites on occasion and graveyard assemblages (as well as church sites) were destroyed at St John the Evangelist, St Martin-in-Balliva and St Botolph in 1962, 1970 and 1974 respectively. The assemblage at St Margaret *in combusto* was excavated, however, partly in 1973 and extensively in 1987.

It was observed above (p.86) that this graveyard came into use about 1100. It developed a particular function, however, as the suffix to the church dedication makes clear: St Margaret *ubi sepeliuntur suspensi* ('where those who have been hanged are buried'). The common gallows stood outside the Magdalen Gate, the churchyard being only some 100m inside the city wall, and it seems very probable that numbers of the skeletons recovered were those of executed criminals.

The normal pattern for Christian burial is for the body to be interred supine (that is, on the back) with the head to the west and the feet to the east. This was the predominant pattern at the graveyard of St Margaret but some burials were interred in a reversed fashion, east-to-west; others were buried prone (that is, face down); some were buried north-to-south; and some had clearly been thrown into pits with little ceremony. Quite frequently individuals in pits or prone had their hands behind their backs, implying that they were tied (*colour plate 15*).

It seems likely that many of these were criminals who had been hanged. Occasionally skeletons were located where it is clear that the body was fully clothed at burial. Buckles and fragments of cloth with eyelets for lacing survived. Bodies tended to be stripped for burial and these clothed individuals could therefore be execution victims. It is also possible, however, that some at least were the victims of plague or epidemic. There were a number of group burials which might imply as much, including one group where seven individuals were interred in a single pit, laid out top-to-toe alternately. A further group of individuals was interred with the arms of the bodies around each other. Most burials remained discrete but this was a poor parish, probably the poorest in the city, and no individual could afford an expensive imported stone coffin. At least one, however, was buried within a grave which had been lined with flint and mortar to give the impression of a freestone coffin.

This skeletal assemblage is very important because it is a large group from a relatively short-use cemetery (it went out of use by the end of the fifteenth century) and it contains individuals who died in the prime of life, either from execution or disease. It thus provides extraordinarily useful data as the results of analysis have demonstrated. Pathologies include Paget's disease, leprosy and, most significantly, treponemal disease or syphilis, evidence that a form of this disease was present in Europe prior to Columbus' discovery of America.

It is also encouraging to note, however, that at least one man may have got away. In 1345 Henry, son of John le Satere, was hanged for felony. Thomas Davy, a clerk, cut him down and took him to St Margaret for burial 'as is the custom'. Before he could be buried, however, Henry revived, presumably because Davy had cut him down too soon. Davy was imprisoned for his pains although the further fate of Henry remains unknown.

THE LATER CASTLE

Henry may well have been tried at the Shirehall as he was hanged at the castle which is where the Shirehall was situated. The earliest record to the *Curia Comitatus* is in 1287 and it stood on Castle Hill, probably within the south bailey. It was built of stone and was in ruins by the reign of Elizabeth. There is a suggestion that it stood on its own low mound which perhaps explains why no trace of it was found in recent extensive excavations. Landscaping in the eighteenth and nineteenth centuries would have removed the mound and with it any residual elements of the building.

The landscaping could not, however, eradicate the massive defensive improvements to the castle which were undertaken in the later twelfth or early thirteenth century. Possibly inspired by the fall of the complex to Prince Louis, Dauphin of France, in 1216 (it was taken without a siege), the castle was re-fortified by the construction of a ditch some 12m (39ft) deep and 27m (88ft) wide across the south bailey in front of the mound. On the inside of this ditch stood a large defensive gateway of flint with limestone dressings. Demolished between the sixteenth and eighteenth centuries, substantial fragments of masonry survived to the north of the ditch, one containing recesses for the hinge supports of a great door, another traces of a window or doorway.

The plan of the gateway could not be recovered, as all the foundations and foundation trenches were destroyed by the cutting of a road in 1862. However,

51 Excavation of the 'barbican' ditch in 1990 (NAU Archaeology)

it seems clear from one of the large surviving fragments that it contained a central passageway with two chambers to one side at least and presumably a similar arrangement on the other side. North of the gateway, a large well was discovered, 2.5m (8ft) square and 30m (97ft) deep, and excavated to a depth of 18m (58ft). This probably provided a defended water supply within the area bounded by the new ditch. The refuse fill contained objects such as a limestone block carved for a game of nine men's morris, the bridge of a musical instrument, a limestone mould for the manufacture of copper alloy belt chapes, two gilded mounts decorated with displayed eagles and material from an armoury including spurs and large numbers of goose wings for fletching arrows.

Other defensive improvements in the thirteenth century included the addition of flanking drum towers at the top of the stone bridge. Set into the mound, the lowest storey of each of these towers survives, complete with its vaulting. In addition, documentary evidence refers to the construction of a perimeter wall of brick around the top of the mound, the bricks being imported from Flanders. This structure seems to have been demolished in the seventeenth century and, despite observations during excavation works on top of the mound, no evidence for its footings has yet been seen.

The castle remained a royal fortification but it was an increasingly anachronistic institution. It may have been besieged in 1174, when the city was attacked by the Flemings (an event that could have been responsible for the scorching of the

52 Excavation of the 'barbican' well in 1991 (NAU Archaeology)

elaborate early Norman vault which survives as a support for part of the now-lost Bigod Tower, the approach tower adjacent to the keep) but, by the early fourteenth century, the defences were in considerable disrepair and some citizens were encroaching upon the castle fee.

As an example, William Bateman, who held property on Timberhill in 1304, was prosecuted for extending his tenement into the King's land. Excavation in 1989 demonstrated that tenement boundaries of properties on Timberhill were extended at this time across the line of the probable fee ditch, encroaching on Crown land. The castle keep was already being used as a gaol in the fourteenth century (a stone survives with a graffito of thirteenth- or fourteenth-century date which reads 'Bartholomew for the truth, wrongfully, and without reason, am I confined in this prison') and, in 1345, the castle area was transferred to the city (except for the mound and the Shirehall) in the second charter of Edward III.

The city maintained the castle 'ditches', as the area was called, as open space, licensing the grazing of animals. There were a number of other areas of such space within the walled circuit. To the north was Gildencroft; much of the area around the church of St Margaret *in combusto* was certainly open land; the cathedral close encompassed much open space, while the prior's fee also included *Cowholme*, summer pasture next to the river; tenting grounds for stretching cloth lay in St Giles parish; Newgate or Surrey Street was probably only built up as far as All Saints' Green and thereafter was open land; and the Butter Hills, inside the southern defences, were also open space.

THE FRIARS

Some of this open land began to be colonised by religious institutions in the thirteenth century. The first friars, Franciscans, arrived in the city in 1226. They gained a large site, to the east of the castle, on land which had been occupied in the Saxo-Norman period but had either been depopulated in the aftermath of the Conquest or was cleared for the friary. A church, that of St John the Evangelist, was taken over by the friars and closed, the parish being added to that of St Peter Parmentergate about 1300. The site of the precinct extended towards the river to the east and was served by a stream, the Dallingfleet. This was bridged with a stone bridge which survived as late as 1888 and may survive still beneath the modern roadway.

Save for fragments of boundary walls, nothing remains of the friary above ground but excavations in 1992/93 revealed that substantial structures and deposits survive below ground. The site was markedly steeper than is indicated by present day topography with noticeable changes in level. The church buildings stood where the upper end of Prince of Wales Road (an 1860s street) stands but south of this were the cloisters and claustral buildings. Excavations uncovered footings of these including a possible kitchen and the walks of the cloisters (*colour plate 9*).

South of the claustral buildings, a substantial flint wall, almost 2m (6ft) high and over 60m (195ft) long, ran west-to-east, apparently dividing the buildings from the gardens, orchards and allotments on the southern perimeter of the precinct. To the north, it was only possible to excavate part of the south wall of the church, the remainder lying beneath the modern road and buildings. However, analysis of documentary evidence has enabled the broad plan to be established, including an understanding of circulation within the precinct.

North of the church, an extant wall behind nineteenth-century structures on Prince-of-Wales Road seems to incorporate elements of another internal friary wall, separating the area of the church from the friary graveyard. One hundred and twenty-four graves were uncovered when the site was excavated in 1998 with a further six recovered in earlier evaluation excavation the previous year. Unsurprisingly, of 92 adult skeletons excavated, 76 were adult males but there were also females and children. Indeed, a third of the skeletal assemblage represented individuals who died before adulthood. It is known that friary cemeteries were often popular with the local urban lay population and burials other than friars can therefore be expected. A gilded silver annular brooch, one of the finest to be recovered from medieval Norwich and decorated with relief

53 Culverts excavated on the site of the site of the Franciscan Friary (NAU Archaeology)

flowers and leaves, a dog chasing a hare, and an inscription reading Jesus of Nazareth King of the Jews, was found at the friary site. It could have been worn by either a man or a woman and, given its ostentation, is more likely to have belonged to a secular individual than a friar.

The Franciscan friary was notable in that, from 1336, it supported a *studium* for the teaching of theology, one of seven such *studia* in England. This was located in the claustral buildings south of the friary church and had a library. The 1992-93 excavations recovered a number of book fittings including a small fourteenth-century copper-alloy page holder decorated with arms of the Clare and Despencer families. Students of the *studium* were not only English but came also from Austria, Italy, Saxony and Westphalia.

The Dominicans also arrived in 1226 and settled north of the river off Colegate. Their site embraced the church of St John the Baptist which was closed and amalgamated with St George Colegate in the thirteenth century. After 1307, however, the Dominicans acquired a more central site south of the river although the Colegate site was retained and used again in the fifteenth century. Nothing now remains above ground north of the river save possibly a fragment of the eastern precinct wall which truncates probable early medieval tenements running back from Magdalen Street. However, substantial later medieval structures survive on the post-1307 site, the most complete friary complex in the country.

This survival, predominantly of fifteenth-century structures, is due to the city purchasing the precinct in 1540. In so doing, the city also acquired the friary archives, including the deeds of properties which went to make up the precinct. It is thus possible to reconstruct the process whereby the Dominicans acquired land and to determine the approximate layout of pre-friary topography. Tenement histories of late thirteenth- and early fourteenth-century date can be compiled, with the last owner before the friars frequently being a man called William But. It is difficult to escape the conclusion that he was acting as an agent for the friars, acquiring property on their behalf as they were not supposed to engage in property transactions. The abuttals on many of the deeds allow the tenements to be grouped geographically so that an idea of the urban complexity of the area can be established.

Despite the fact that the Dominicans were establishing a precinct on such an urban area, the northern part of their site was marginal land, low-lying and adjacent to the river. Excavations in the cloister, which lay to the north of the church, in 1974 and again in 1992 have revealed the massive dumping of rubbish material which was necessary in order to raise the land here to allow building.

The Carmelites or White Friars established their friary in 1256. It too was built on marginal land and stood next to the river, north of Whitefriars Bridge. As with most of the other precincts, the site is largely destroyed above ground. Foundations of a building interpreted as the church were observed in 1904 and

54 Excavations at the Carmelite friary showing the east walk of the cloister with burials below the walkway (Brian Ayers)

Left: 55 Detail of pier bases to support the cloister arcade at the Carmelite Friary (Brian Ayers)

Below: 56 Detail of the Arminghall Arch, now in Norwich Magistrates' Courts (Brian Ayers)

skeletons were found during building works in the 1950s and 1960s (including a rare late fourteenth-century rectangular oak coffin). An arch survives close to St Martin's or Whitefriars Bridge. Further north, a vaulted undercroft also stands, the walls of which date to the fourteenth century.

Until 2002, the only modern controlled excavation of the site was that undertaken in 1976 within the undercroft (locating traces of pre-friary deposits, including a timber-framed but clay-walled building). Comprehensive redevelopment has now enabled large-scale excavation to be carried out which has revolutionised earlier ideas concerning the layout of the friary. The friary church was revealed to have been a substantial structure with north and south aisles, standing at the southern extremity of the site, dominating the bridge over the river and as close as possible to the centre of the city. The surviving arch was a doorway into the church. The cloisters, 100ft (31m) square stood to the north with the extant undercroft forming part of the north range of the cloister next to the north claustral walk. Excavation demonstrated that it had continued to the east but was truncated and a blocking wall inserted.

The east walk was uncovered entirely by the excavation with well-preserved sleeper walls to the garth linking the bases of the piers for the claustral arcade. The sleeper walls and piers were dressed with a limestone plinth, above which the rubble core was faced with squared-and-knapped flintwork. Floor tile impressions and occasional plain tiles themselves were recorded and burials had been cut at regular intervals along the length of the walk.

The east range of the cloister was also well-preserved and contained a heated room although the hearth and its associated stack may have been inserted at a late date. East of this range stood a further, smaller cloister, re-surfaced in the post-medieval period and thus re-used. It is illustrated on nineteenth-century maps of the city and served to confuse earlier attempts to understand the complex. Material from the site is currently being analysed but it includes large numbers of copper alloy book mounts, indicative once again of friaries as centres of learning.

The most extraordinary survival from the friary, however, is no longer on the site. This is an early fourteenth-century arch of limestone with vine leaf decoration, carved dragons and other beasts, the head of a bearded man at the apex, and with flanking female figures and kings set within smaller arched niches. Although known to have been set within a porch at Arminghall Old Hall, south of Norwich, from the sixteenth century until 1910, the arch was almost certainly removed from the friary at the time of the Reformation. It has now been returned to Norwich and re-erected inside the Magistrates' Courts, on the south bank of the river opposite the site of the friary. The original function of this arch is difficult to determine but it has been argued that it formed a gateway or a porch.

The fourth great friary was that of the Austin Friars. They settled in Norwich in 1290 on a large site next to the Wensum off King Street. They too took over the site of a church (St Michael Conesford) and closed it about 1360. Little remains of the precinct save part of the north-eastern boundary wall. The area was subjected to massive development in 1970 with only minimal recording possible by two undergraduates from the University of East Anglia. The site was sloping which enhanced the preservation of buried walls and these were found standing in excess of two metres in height across the area. They were all swept away but the site is once again ready for redevelopment. Evaluation work has established that elements of the friary still survive well, albeit not to a height of 2m but occasionally in excess of 1m.

The restricted work to date has uncovered a substantial wall which is tentatively considered to form the north wall of the church. Within, the wall is plastered and burials survive below a floor surface with tile impressions. Small excavations have also been undertaken adjacent to Howard House, a seventeenth-century structure in the north-western corner of the precinct. These have revealed medieval fabric, increasing the possibility, first promoted by Andy Shelley, that the house may have been formed out of the remains of the friary gatehouse.

Other friars also settled in Norwich. The Sack Friars were established about 1254 but their order was suppressed in 1307 and their site passed to the Dominicans. The Pied Friars were also suppressed in 1307 and their house, to the north of the churchyard of St Peter Parmentergate, became a college of priests linked to the hospital of Beck in Billingford, Norfolk. The north wall of 72 King Street appears to have formed part of this college, being incorporated into a seventeenth-century cottage. Friars of Our Lady seem to have lived south of the church of St Julian and, for a while, Carmelites were established within a house in the churchyard of St Martin in Balliva, close to the castle.

HOSPITALS AND COLLEGES

The establishment of friaries was augmented by the establishment of further hospitals. The greatest of these was the Hospital of St Giles, or the Great Hospital, on Bishopgate, founded in 1249 by Walter Suffield, Bishop of Norwich for 'the infirm poor' and 'poor priests'. Built upon the low-lying pasture of Cowholme to the north-east of the cathedral, the marginal land of the site symbolised the position of such hospitals 'as brokers between heaven and earth'. The institution is notable for the range of later medieval buildings which survive and for its extraordinary documentation. It was a modest establishment in the thirteenth century, its chapel probably also providing the parochial functions of the nearby church of St Helen after 1270 when the master and brethen acquired this church and demolished it. The other foundation was Hildebrond's Hospital, a common hall for poor people established by Hildebrond and his wife Maud in 1216. This stood in the southern ward of Conesford and was subsequently attached to the church of St Edward but nothing now remains of either.

57 The Great Hospital (Brian Ayers)

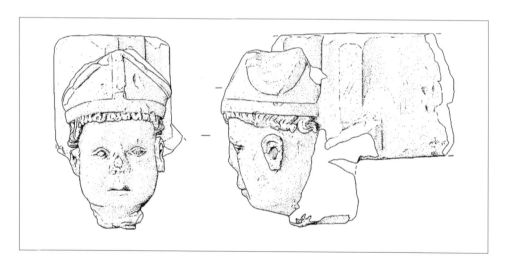

58 Label stop depicting a bishop (Steven Ashley)

While there were numerous additional small ecclesiastical foundations throughout the city, the other great thirteenth-century establishment was that of the College of St Mary in the Fields. This was founded about 1250 and stood in the western part of the city, close to the churches of St Peter Mancroft and St Stephen. It functioned as a community of priests and had its own church with a cloister and claustral buildings. Although largely destroyed at the Reformation, elements of it survive within the fabric of the later Assembly House (including an undercroft) and the broad plan of the establishment is known. Refurbishment at the adjacent Theatre Royal necessitated the demolition of a wall within which was located a carved label stop depicting a bishop. This fourteenth-century carving was almost certainly from the college and may represent a benefactor.

The early statutes of the Great Hospital enjoined it to support seven 'poor scholars'. Two schools are known, both associated with the cathedral priory. The first of these is mentioned in a papal bull of 1156 and lay outside the cathedral close to the north, next to the river. The school buildings appear to have survived the Reformation, being demolished after 1568. The site is cleared and awaiting redevelopment. A second school was the cathedral Almonry School which probably prepared boys for the Benedictine priory. A reference to this school in 1311 is the earliest such reference in England.

Not all institutional development was ecclesiastical. A toll-house was also established in the thirteenth century on the Market Place. It stood on the site of the existing Guildhall and, as well as being used to collect tolls, it also acted as a law court and prison. A reference of 1276 to *(in prisona) tholonii Norwici* indicates this dual function.

It would be a mistake, however, to view the history of Norwich in the thirteenth and early fourteenth centuries as one of unalloyed growth and success. There were setbacks, some considerable. It has already been noted that the castle fell to the Dauphin of France in 1216. In 1266 rebellious barons called 'The Disinherited' raided Norwich and reputedly carried off 140 carts of loot. The most far-reaching incident was probably the riot of 1272 when the citizens, apparently under extreme provocation from the prior, attacked the cathedral precinct, burning down the Ethelbert Gate and St Ethelbert's church, sacking the cloisters and also burning much of the cathedral church. The King himself came to Norwich to restore order. The effects of the fire can still be seen on the Ethelbert Gate and in parts of the cathedral while St Ethelbert's church was never rebuilt, being replaced by a chapel in the new gateway. The stone building excavated at St Martin-at-Palace Plain was apparently destroyed at about this time; as it was a cathedral property outside the protection of the precinct, it may have been one of the first to suffer in the riot. It would remain a ruin for over 100 years.

Despite such events, Norwich by the 1340s was a greatly enhanced city with a burgeoning population, increasing wealth and major secular and ecclesiastical institutions. It had weathered setbacks to emerge as the dominant city of East Anglia with a commercial network which embraced local, regional, national and international trade. Disaster, however, was lying in wait.

6

FROM BLACK DEATH
TO GREAT FIRE

About 1377 the parish of St Mathew, a small church immediately outside the north wall of the cathedral close, was added to that of St Martin-at-Palace. It had suffered grievously at the time of the Black Death in 1349 and had never recovered. In this it was not alone: the parish of St Catherine or St Winwaloy in the southern part of the city seems to have become completely depopulated; St Anne on King Street was added to St Clement Conesford about 1370; and depopulation seems to have led to the disuse of St Margaret New Bridge, where the chancel came to serve as a hermitage for a hermit charged with looking after the bridge.

It is probable that pestilence in the mid-fourteenth century claimed as many as one in three of the population, consistent with evidence from elsewhere in the country. In the short term the effect upon the economy of Norwich must have been intense although this is difficult to assess in the material evidence which survives, other than in losses of marginal churches such as St Catherine or St Margaret. The church at New Bridge was almost certainly one of the latest to be founded in Norwich, on reclaimed land next to the Wensum. Its endowment must have been small and it was therefore vulnerable at times of stress.

The city seems, nevertheless, to have recovered rapidly. Interestingly, although there were further church losses in the fifteenth century (usually as a result of amalgamation of parishes), generally the number remained fairly static. Indeed, by the late fourteenth century, the evidence of the surviving churches seems to indicate a renewal of investment rather than retrenchment. Building additions, in the form either of added aisles or chantries, become common throughout the city, paving the way for massive rebuilding campaigns of certain churches in the fifteenth century. As examples, the chancel of St Gregory was rebuilt in 1394 (wall paintings depicting the four doctors of the church werer uncovered in the south chancel aisle recently – see *colour plate 24*) and the aisles of St Martin-at-Palace date from the late fourteenth century, as does the lower section of the tower of St Stephen.

St Gregory's chancel was built at the expense of the cathedral priory but much other investment in churches seems to have been the result of private benefaction. Many older merchant families disappear from records at the time of the Black Death, but late fourteenth-century Norwich was still a city which contained wealthy individuals and these did not hesitate to display their wealth at home as well as at church, producing monuments which still stand.

THE URBAN ÉLITE

As early as 1370, the father of William Appleyard, the first mayor of Norwich, probably built the house now known as the Bridewell. It occupies a block of property between two streets, with the house itself set back from the street frontages. The building, one of the 18 late medieval secular houses to survive in Norwich, was constructed on a grand scale with a suite of vaulted undercrofts beneath its northern and eastern ranges. The public face of the north range is a *tour-de-force* of squared and knapped flint, most probably the wall seen by Celia Fiennes in 1698.

Other such houses include Strangers' Hall (now a museum, like the Bridewell). This began as a fourteenth-century hall at right-angles to the street, above an early brick-vaulted undercroft with stone ribs. It was rebuilt in courtyard style

59 North wall of William Appleyard's house (Brian Ayers)

in the fifteenth century with the hall parallel to the street although retaining the undercroft. Quoins of the fourteenth-century building can be seen in the courtyard, as can quoins of a further building in the yard of the Plough Inn on St Benedict's Street. Elsewhere, excavations have uncovered the footings of a fourteenth-century house of more modest pretensions at St Martin-at-Palace Plain (supplementing records made in 1962 when it was demolished).

These are all grand structures of an affluent élite, many of whose members operated as an oligarchy controlling the city. Recent detailed study of the surviving houses by Chris King has not only explored how these buildings developed but also how they were used and their probable role within urban society. Norwich is unusual in having few late medieval guildhalls, meaning that entertainment had to take place within inns or, more probably, private houses. Such use could easily lead to exclusion and the rise of factionalism for which the city was notorious in the fifteenth century. An archaeological approach to the architecture of these buildings is therefore assisting understanding of élite social and political activity in Norwich as well as revealing more subtle 'signals' to the observer: at Stranger's Hall, the fifteenth-century refurbishment initiated by Nicholas Sotherton was incomplete at his death and was finished by his widow,

60 Boss in porch of Strangers Hall showing widow's head (Brian Ayers)

Agnes. The female head wearing a widow's veil on the central boss of the porch vault may well depict Agnes, providing a statement that she was now head of the household.

In many ways the development of the power of the urban oligarchy defined the development of the city as a distinct institution. Recognition of the oligarchy's power and importance came in 1404, when the city acquired the right to self-government through a mayor and aldermen. This was, however, more of a formalisation of a growing sense of corporate identity which can be traced back to at least the thirteenth century. Corporate ownership and responsibility for property, for instance, dated from at least 1250, as the construction of communal defences illustrates. Acquisition of the castle fee and extension of city control over wasteland in 1345 extended holdings and, after the Black Death, the wealth of the late fourteenth-century city was also to be made manifest in public buildings and corporate control.

Initially such increases to the corporate portfolio were acquisitions. The city bought up shops and market stalls and controlled the sale of meat, poultry and fish. In 1379 the Old and New Common Staiths were acquired on King Street in order to control goods and shipping. Nothing remains of either above ground but a contract exists from 1432 when the city agreed with one John Marwe for him to replace an old wooden staith and build 'the new comon kaye of Norwich'. The contract is detailed, stipulating a foundation of oak piles with a quay of freestone above.

In 1384 the city acquired a large site north of the Market Place to act as a Cloth Seld or public hall for the sealing and control of cloth (it also acted as a hostel for foreign merchants). It is likely that large parts of this building (or a sixteenth-century successor) survived until 1963 when it was pulled down without record (it is thought that the range on the Pottergate frontage was 31ft [9.5m] wide). Much of the area is, nevertheless, still a rabbit warren of structures, many of which could contain elements of this important building.

At the end of the fourteenth century, the city undertook the first of several major building initiatives. A tower known as the *donjon* or Dungeon Tower, in the angle of the river Wensum, had been acquired from the Great Hospital in 1378 (although the documentary evidence is less than clear-cut). A remarkable document in the Chamberlains' Roll of 1398-9, however, indicates that the tower was completely rebuilt at this date, producing the structure which stand to the present day, known as the Cow Tower (*colour plate 16*).

The building was surveyed in 1985-6 and is interpreted as a freestanding artillery tower, with gun emplacements on the roof and loops for hand guns within embrasures on the first and second floors. It was furnished with latrines and hearths and, probably, a vaulted undercroft. Faced in brick (almost all of which survives), the core of the fabric contains large quantities of flint. The tower provided defence for the city at a vulnerable spot where the river is overlooked by the high ground of

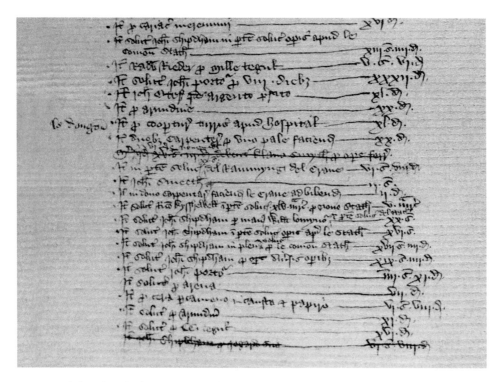

61 Part of the Chamberlains' Account for 1398/99 detailing payments at the Cow Tower (Norfolk & Norwich Record Office/Norfolk Museums & Archaeology Service)

Mousehold Heath, and was connected to the fortified Bishop Bridge (to the south) and the city (to the west) by a palisade which ran along the river bank.

The Chamberlains' Roll is valuable not only for dating the construction of the Cow Tower but also for the detail it provides concerning the processes involved and the materials needed. It lists the workmen, the days worked and payments made for miscellaneous items. Carters, carpenters, masons and labourers all worked on the tower, while payments were also made to stone-miners who must have supplied the flint. Bricks were bought from a variety of sources and small items were also recorded: 1d for the carriage of a *cabyll*; 10d for the hire of a boat at various times to carry *hirdeles*; 2d for a *Wyndynhook* for the windlass; 6d for a *barell*; 6d to make four *tubbes* from the said *barell*; and 19d for 'payments for drink at various times'. The total account, which was rendered in Latin with the exception of occasional words in English as italicised here, was £36 17s 2½d.

The Cow Tower was clearly a major undertaking and is unique in that such a comprehensive documentary account survives for a building so little altered. The city oligarchy was soon involved in further considerable expenditure. A new guildhall was erected on the site of the old tollhouse between 1407 and 1412. Designed as one of the most splendid of provincial guildhalls, this also still stands (although drastically 'restored' in the 1860s) with a fine example of East Anglian flint diaperwork on the exterior east façade (*colour plate 22*). The building is situated on a sloping site above a vaulted undercroft. It consisted of a council chamber or mayor's court, now with a roof of 1534-7, an assembly chamber designed for meetings of the full medieval council and a 'free prison' on the ground floor (for unchained prisoners). The vaulted undercroft provided a more secure prison. Its door, which can only be opened from the outside, also survives.

Other early fifteenth-century expenditure included a new Market Cross in 1411 (this was replaced in 1501-03). Construction of city watermills at New Mills was completed in 1410 but problems with the sluices led to serious flooding in the suburb of Heigham upstream and the mills were not effectively operational until 1430. They defined the head of the Wensum as they straddled the river and are illustrated as housed within a timber-framed structure on a plan of 1541; the site is now occupied by a fine nineteenth-century pumping station.

The corporate body of the city was therefore a major element in Norwich society by the beginning of the fifteenth century. The city was able to act increasingly as an independent institution (although riots in the 1430s and 1440s twice led to brief seizure by the King). This independence may have assisted the more affluent against the less wealthy. It is clear from various documentary sources that the oligarchy was not universally popular. In addition, given that in the fifteenth century the wealth of the city overall seems to have been in decline, the fact that many of the major surviving medieval structures were built or rebuilt at this time emphasises that the great merchant class still had disposable income, presumably at the expense of their neighbours.

BUILDINGS

The buildings which resulted from the disposal of this income were both domestic and ecclesiastical. As mentioned above, some 18 of the former survive, some only recognised in the relatively recent past. One such is the Old Barge or Dragon Hall on King Street, effectively re-discovered after 1979 with the gradual removal of later partitions and subsequently surveyed. Recently, this survey has been updated and supplemented by comprehensive excavation at the rear of the property (*colour plates 1 and 10*). Together with documentary research, it is now possible to see a building complex assembled from a combination of existing structures and new build in about 1427. It is likely that the person responsible was an affluent merchant called Robert Toppes although, if so, he achieved the feat at the precocious age of 22.

The principal structure at Dragon Hall is a street frontage range which extends the length of combined properties between St Ann's Lane and Old Barge Yard. Its

62 Spandrel at Dragon Hall (Kirk Laws-Chapman)

ground floor consists, in large part, of earlier fabric, re-used to carry a massive timber-framed first floor hall parallel to and running the length of the street frontage. This hall is surmounted by a crown-post roof with one of its spandrels (a triangular area formed by a brace running from the wall-post to a tie-beam) containing an openwork painted carving of a dragon (hence the modern name of the building: there is evidence that other spandrels also contained carvings). The front elevation is slightly jettied, with a surviving decorated corbel at the southern end. At the rear of the building, there is a wider jetty supported by posts and which thus enabled provision of a covered open-air arcaded passage towards the river.

At its southern end, the arcaded passage links with a screens passage associated with an earlier hall wing which lies behind the street frontage and at right-angles to it. The service rooms of this earlier hall were removed with construction of the street range and ground floor levels raised, in part to allow the insertion of a brick-vaulted undercroft. A new doorway, to one side of the blocked service doors, was constructed from the screens passage into the ground floor of the street range. From there a stair, now lost but replaced by a modern example, led to the first floor.

The rear arcade includes a large timber arch facing the river which stands at the top of a sloping lane leading down to the waterfront. Prior to the construction of

Dragon Hall, this lane had led from a large brick arch within a boundary wall which was set back from the street frontage. The arch and wall were retained in the new build, the wall providing the back wall of the street range and the arch providing direct access to the ground floor of the structure (*via* the timber arch) from the river. The earlier boundary wall was not aligned parallel to the street; its re-use means that the ground floor of the building is irregular in shape although the timber-framed first floor and the arcade posts are set in a more rectangular manner. As a result, the arcaded passage narrows to the north as the earlier wall tapers eastward.

The major fifteenth-century rebuilding which is Dragon Hall must have been associated with river traffic and trade and, indeed, Toppes is known to have been an affluent cloth merchant with extensive landholdings in north Norfolk. The first-floor hall was divided into two parts and it is thought that the northern end, served by the arches, would have acted as a display and selling area for cloth, with the more private southern end being used for business transactions and domestic matters.

Dragon Hall is only one building on King Street to have been refurbished in the fifteenth century. The Music House, the twelfth-century hall of the Jews Jurnet and Isaac, also had a brick-vaulted undercroft inserted within the street range south of the chamber block. The building was refurbished upstairs too, including the insertion of a scissor-brace roof. This probably came from demolition of a wider building elsewhere; the prefabrication numbering system on the timber was ignored, the roof being inserted to fit the existing walls with earlier mortice joints in the underside of the rafters remaining unused.

At St Martin-at-Palace Plain, the twelfth-century stone building, which was probably demolished in the late thirteenth century, was brought back into use by the creation of a vault of brick above three inserted piers of brick and flint. The vault had to be 'crippled' around existing apertures and corbels survived in the walls to show where ribs to effect this crippling had run. This new vault supported a timber-framed building, glimpses of which can be seen behind a Georgian façade in photographs of the 1940s. It was demolished by 1956.

Other fifteenth-century houses were new-built. Among these are two distinctive buildings on the north bank of the river. The first is the west range of Bacon House on the corner of St George's Street and Colegate; it consists of a rare stone-faced hall parallel to and upon the street frontage. The other is the street range of a building only discovered in 1988 and subsequently restored on Fye Bridge Street and now known as The King of Hearts. It forms the only other known fifteenth-century domestic building to be aligned along the street. A further fifteenth-century building is Suckling House on St Andrew's Street. This structure has a high crown-post and scissor-brace roof with a brick bay window (reconstructed in the twentieth century) facing a small courtyard. Service rooms stand at the west end, beyond a lost screens passage marked by surviving opposed doors. In addition there was a stair turret (now lost) and, to the north, a courtyard and a further range destroyed by the construction of a tramway at the end of the nineteenth century.

The nearest parallel to Suckling House is Stranger's Hall, itself noted above as rebuilt in the fifteenth century incorporating earlier elements. Here, by the late fifteenth century, the hall lay parallel to and set back from the street, separated by a surviving courtyard and street frontage range. It too has a bay window, here constructed in stone. Early access was by a southern single storey stair turret but this was abandoned within the fifteenth century for access by an open stair from the courtyard to the north.

Other, demolished, fifteenth-century structures are known including a building which survived on Quayside until 1962. This was the New Star Inn, a rare example of a fifteenth-century merchant's house and warehouse. Its site has not been excavated, other than for a rapid trench in 1962 itself which uncovered evidence for an earlier shell fishery, but excavated examples of such buildings of quality are now beginning to be uncovered. Work on King Street in 1999 at the Ben Burgess site uncovered a similar building to Dragon Hall, that is a hall at right angles to the street behind a street range, complete with a cesspit furnished with a chute through the wall.

Windows were clearly important features of the houses of the affluent at this time. A fourteenth-century house at Palace Plain had a bay window added in the fifteenth century (it was demolished in 1962 but re-erected nearby in 1970) and a similar bay window partly survives at the Great Hall, Oak Street. Slightly later, in the sixteenth century, large windows were used in the rear range of The King of Hearts and also in the rear range of the Plough Inn on St Benedict's Street.

Fireplaces were also grand in the greater houses: side columns of a fifteenth-century example were recovered from St Mary's Plain in 1959. Painted glass and wall paintings are also known: fragments of a painting depicting a knight in armour on horseback survive from the demolished White Swan Inn. Buildings were sometimes adorned with carved wooden brackets as with the figure of a young man, also from the White Swan (one of several – the others disappeared at the time of demolition), or the sixteenth-century example still in place on Garsett House, St Andrew's Hall Plain.

These buildings are all exceptional structures in that, firstly, examples survive and that, secondly, they represent the most affluent level in medieval urban society. As such they are atypical, but all domestic buildings of less affluent groups have disappeared (even Pykerell's House on St Mary's Plain, one of the smallest surviving fifteenth-century buildings, is a house of quality). It is only possible to recover the plan and history of the vast remainder through excavation. This was done most effectively at Pottergate in 1974 for houses of intermediate status and at Alms Lane in 1976 for poorer structures.

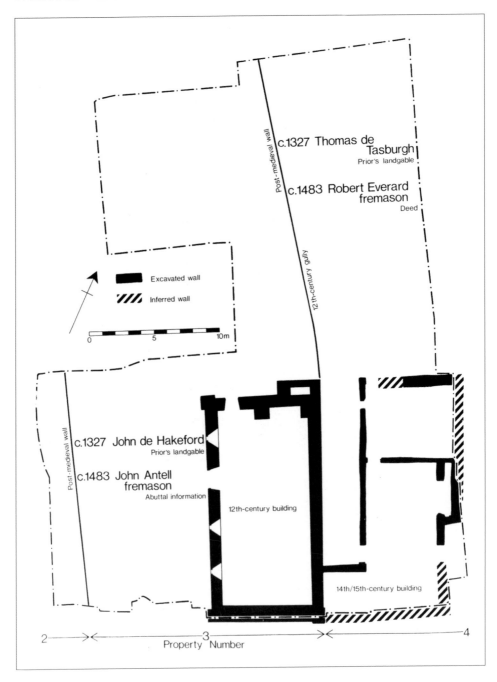

63 Plan of houses at St Martin-at-Palace Plain (Jayne Bown)

64 Excavation of houses
destroyed by fire in 1507
(Norwich Survey)

The site at the corner of Pottergate and St Laurence's Lane was devastated
by fire on 25 March 1507. Three types of house were identified by excavation:
a large single-storied building with a range parallel to the street and a hall to
the rear; a two-storied house with cellars to the rear; and a building range of
late fifteenth-century date on the Pottergate frontage, probably divided into
three houses All these were destroyed and not rebuilt until the seventeenth
century. The cellars were roofed in timber and the collapse of the buildings
above also entailed the collapse of much of the contents of the houses into the
cellars. Excavation therefore recovered not only evidence of the structures but
also a dated collection of contents, helping to determine the social status of the
occupants.

It is clear that the buildings did not house the urban poor. The cellar walls were
of flint with brick quoins. Lamp niches and windows were also fashioned in brick.
Cellar windows would have been in the north wall where the land fell away; here
too was a stair to the ground floor, also of brick with treads of quartered tree trunks.

Cesspits provided sanitation, one at least being fed by a chute. It is probable that each of the three buildings in the single range was gable-end on to the street and of two storeys (structures likely to have been similar in style and scale to the only surviving – much altered – gable-to-end medieval house in Norwich at No. 8 Tombland). Each probably had timber-framed party walls with ground floor walls of flint rubble and brick and was heated, perhaps by stoves as fragments of stove-tile were recovered, the earliest evidence in England for the use of closed stoves. The easternmost house may have had hearths of plain and glazed Flemish floor tiles.

The contents of the cellars were particularly rich in kitchen equipment and including cooking pots, a skillet, fragments of a colander, a long-handled cooking pan, a skimmer, a strike-a-light and part of a spit. Other finds included candlesticks, painted glass, horticultural implements, a terracotta plaque which possibly depicts St John the Baptist, and door furniture. The buildings were small in scale but well built and their contents suggest that the occupants were comparatively affluent. The discoveries seem to demonstrate the sort of structure that reasonably prosperous citizens could expect to inhabit in the late fifteenth century without the ostentation of the great courtyard houses of the truly wealthy.

Excavations at Alms Lane in 1976 uncovered evidence for more modest dwellings. Here, buildings of the first half of the fifteenth century were constructed with clay walls, occasionally interspersed with timber posts, were of one storey and of two rooms. In only one building was there any trace of heating by a hearth.

These structures largely continued in use in the second half of the century, clay again being used for walls although the addition of timbers in one structure is interpreted as being to allow the construction of a loft. Floors were generally of clay and may have been covered with rush matting. Heating was becoming more common with hearths being constructed next to walls and furnished with a simple chimney or hood. Rubbish disposal seems to have been rudimentary; only one cesspit was located and this was a clay-lined pit rather than a stone construction as at Pottergate.

The vast majority of the population would have occupied buildings similar to those at Alms Lane. Although such structures could exist side by aside with more affluent buildings (the fifteenth-century wing of Bacon House stands across the road from the Alms Lane site), most of the better houses were in the richest parishes of the heart of the city, those of SS Andrew, Giles, Peter Mancroft and Stephen.

UNDERCROFTS

This much can be gleaned from the documentation (all the goldsmiths in fourteenth-century Norwich lived in the parish of St Peter Mancroft for example) but more material evidence is available in the structures of the city. While nearly all of the medieval secular buildings have been lost, undercrofts built beneath them by the merchant class frequently survive. These structures, built of brick and flint and, by virtue of their design, wholly or partly buried, often escaped fires and demolition intact and were re-used in later buildings. Many that were not re-used are discovered by excavation (usually although not always without their vaults) or were bricked up and survive sealed.

Over 60 such undercrofts, almost all of them of fifteenth-century date, are known to exist within Norwich and the sites of over 30 others are known. Most are on the south bank of the river Wensum, exploiting hillside sites in, generally, the four most affluent parishes of the city. They were frequently built into the hill, providing a platform for house construction above but with ground-floor access to the cellar at the lower part of the slope.

Most of the undercrofts have rectangular plans with walls of flint. The roofs can be groined or barrel-vaulted with the provision of ribs, wall arches, axial piers and side chambers as necessary. Ribs and webbing are of brick with little variation in rib form. Lamp niches are usually located in the walls, fashioned in brick and frequently opposite the entrance. Many undercrofts can be accessed from within the building, usually by a stair of brick although this is not always

65 Part of vaulted undercroft at Strangers' Hall (Kirk Laws-Chapman)

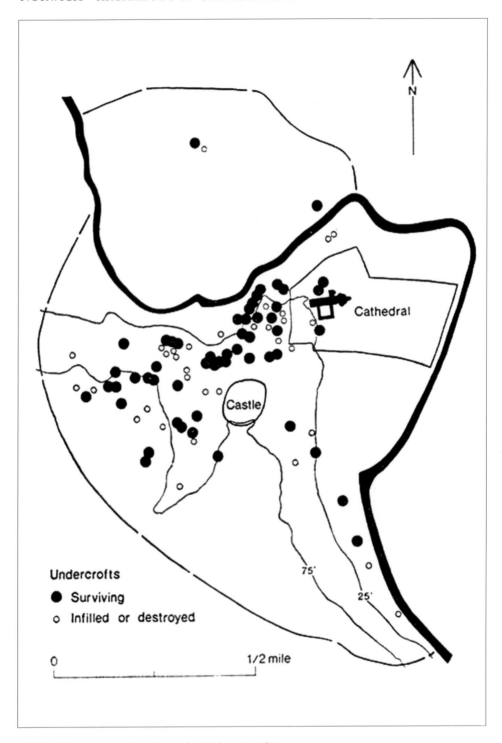

N

Cathedral

Castle

Undercrofts

● Surviving

○ Infilled or destroyed

75'

25'

0   1/2 mile

66 Distribution map of undercrofts (Robert Smith)

the case; some could be entered by external doors, normally from the side or rear of the property.

The single largest suite of undercrofts is that below the Bridewell Museum which dates in part to the late fourteenth century. The complex plan ultimately comprised an L-shaped undercroft which began with ten compartments of vaulting arranged around three central piers and two bays around a central lateral rib. This stood beneath the hall and service rooms. Two separate additions extended the undercroft suite to the west with octopartite vaulting. Deviations in the rib patterns indicate missing doorways and windows (the undercrofts are only partly below ground) and where an inserted doorway subsequently enabled internal access to what originally had been designed as an undercroft with external access only.

The Bridewell was a grand house but the intensive use of space by undercrofts is found elsewhere such as beneath No. 4 Tombland, where there is a three-bayed undercroft with six side chambers, single-chamfered diagonal ribs and wall arches. A further structure of two bays and an end chamber on Redwell Street is linked by a vaulted side passage, with stairs leading from this passage to a side entrance. Particularly fine undercrofts survived beneath the White Swan – these were broken in by demolition in 1962 although evaluation excavation in 1995 indicated that the walls survived to springing level with demolition debris within the structures suggesting the possibility at least of eventual reconstruction. Occasionally fragments of destroyed undercrofts are located, as beneath the site of the demolished Bird in Hand public house on King Street in 2000 or timber-roofed cellars are located with vaulted side-chambers – one such example was excavated on St Andrew Street in 2002.

Undercrofts are not only extant within secular structures. Probably the finest architectural example within the city is that located within the Dominican friary complex (and now known as the Crypt – it is used as a café). The brick walls probably date from 1258-67, a very early use of brick as a building material, but the vault was added in the fifteenth century. Although restored, it is a high ribbed vault dividing the square crypt into four bays.

Brick vaulting can be seen in another ecclesiastical building, that which forms part of the north range of the cloisters of the Carmelite friary. Here the walls are predominantly fourteenth-century in date but the vault was added in the fifteenth century. Piers of brick were constructed to allow springing of the ribs. Brick vaults also exist beneath the late fourteenth-century cellarer's range at the cathedral, a long north-to-south aligned building on a slope where the vaults enable the first floor to achieve ground floor access on its western side.

BUILDING MATERIALS

The increasingly widespread use of brick in the fifteenth century can be noted throughout the city. The spire of the cathedral, the fourth to be constructed, was built about 1480 by Bishop Goldwell after the third spire was struck by lightening in 1463 (the first, timber, spire was burnt in 1272; its replacement fell in a storm of 1361/62). This fourth spire is of brick encased in stone. Similarly, the piers on the church of St Swithin are rendered and limewashed to give the appearance of stone but are, again, of brick. Stairs in numerous buildings, particularly church porches and as access to towers and rood lofts, are of brick, and drains and conduits were increasingly lined and vaulted in brick. Detailing was undertaken in brick as when refurbishment of the excavated stone building at St Martin-at-Palace Plain necessitated the use of chamfered brick for the window dressings to replace robbed earlier dressings of Barnack limestone.

Brick manufacture may have taken place immediately outside the western wall of the city, as there were brickfields here in the post-medieval period. Much brick could have been imported, probably by water from the eastern part of the county. A last of 'Tyle' (probably 'wall tile', meaning brick) was purchased from St Benet's Abbey on the river Bure in 1388/89 where it is likely that there were brick kilns and tileries. Importation of brick has a long history in Norwich; it was seen above how Flemish bricks were purchased in the 1260s to provide a curtain wall around the top of the mound at the castle.

While bricks, and of course tiles, were needed for building campaigns in the fifteenth century, a greater need was for stone and lime. The houses of the richer merchants used large quantities of flint and mortar but these were still relatively minor amounts compared to those required for major ecclesiastical rebuilding programmes. The church of St Peter Mancroft, the most splendid parish church within Norwich, was entirely rebuilt in the fifteenth century (*colour plate 21*); the Dominican friary was largely destroyed by fire in 1413 and was eventually completed on a grand scale in 1470; the church of St Andrew seems to have been rebuilt completely between 1450 and 1520; and St George Colegate was rebuilt from about 1459 to 1513.

Flint and lime were available in quantity locally and were quarried both within and outside the city walls. A large part of the Ber Street escarpment in the southern area of the walled city, between Ber Street and King Street, was exploited in this way and the steep wooded slopes which still survive here are the remains of a relict industrial landscape. However, the provision of freestone to Norwich was more difficult, the nearest decent freestone coming from Northamptonshire quarries. Nevertheless, those responsible for the greater churches were not thwarted: Mancroft obtained stone from Ancaster and was left 40s in 1506 to pave the chancel in marble; the cathedral, for which stone had been brought from Caen in the eleventh and twelfth centuries, was buying stone in Purbeck, Dublin and Clipsham (Rutland) in the fourteenth century; and excavations at the Franciscan friary have identified Purbeck marble in floorings of probable fifteenth-century date.

Sand and gravel were also quarried. Quantities of these materials were extracted on Mousehold Heath, where an early map depicts 'ston mynes', but there is also increasing evidence for such quarrying from excavation sites in the city centre. Relatively extensive extraction, for example, was being undertaken within the castle precinct before the end of the Middle Ages. This extraction was particularly great against the south-western rampart of the south bailey, so much so that the rampart had to be cut back in the fifteenth century and revetted with a stone wall. Quarry pits have been found recently on Ber Street in 1999, off Cattle Market Street in 2000 and at St Peter's Street in 2001.

The workmen and craftsmen who effected the late fourteenth- and fifteenth-century rebuilding of Norwich remain largely anonymous, although some are known through sources such as the Cow Tower account (a number of labourers are mentioned by name here) or because of their skills. Two masons, Robert Everard and John Antell, occupied adjoining houses at Palace Plain in 1483. Everard worked at the cathedral where he may have provided the nave vault for Bishop Walter Lyhart and was almost certainly responsible for the present spire (William of Worcester made a marginal note about 1478 to ask Everard about the spire). Antell has been recognised as the mason responsible for work at the churches of St George Colegate, St Martin-at-Oak and St Michael Coslany. He seems to have had a workshop on Bishopgate. Evidence for a masons' yard was excavated at the cathedral in 1987, where a deposit of limestone dust and chippings was discovered in an enclosed area north of the nave.

THE CHURCHES

Although archaeological excavation has been helping to clarify the development of secular buildings in late medieval Norwich, results to date on church excavations have been limited. Only one standing church has been submitted to a reasonably thorough excavation – that of St Martin-at-Palace in 1988 – and even here work was largely confined to the nave. Nevertheless, it was possible to establish a sequence of development, despite floor deposits being severely damaged by post-medieval intrusive burial.

More limited work at the church of St James in 1979 was also able to examine a sequence of construction including major rebuilding in the fifteenth century. Excavation in 1972 on the site of the bombed church of St Benedict recovered a sequence of ground plans and, together with documentation and architectural

67 Excavation within the church of
St Martin-at-Palace (NAU Archaeology)

detailing which was either recorded before or survived the bombing, was able
to establish that fifteenth-century alterations included the addition of western
and eastern bays, a chapel and a porch to the north aisle, and the insertion
of a clerestory. The site of the church of St Margaret *in combusto* had been
completely destroyed by cellars and thus was not excavated when its graveyard
was uncovered in 1987; a fragment of window tracery was recovered, however,
from the remains of an adjacent sixteenth-century cellar. Work in 1997 at the
ruined church of St Peter Southgate uncovered the foundations of a fifteenth-
century south porch and part of the south wall.

Archaeological examination of the growth of churches may be limited
(although details of ecclesiastical life have been recovered, such as a fourteenth-
century pewter chalice and paten from the grave of a priest at Carrow Priory)
but considerable information can be gleaned from later medieval wills for works
which were effected in churches. At St Laurence, for instance, bequests were
made for work on the tower in 1468, 1470, 1472, 1473, 1479 and, finally, in
1508 'to fynyshyng of ye stepyll'. In St George Tombland bequests for the roof
were made in 1447 and 1518; one such repair may have led to the curious loss

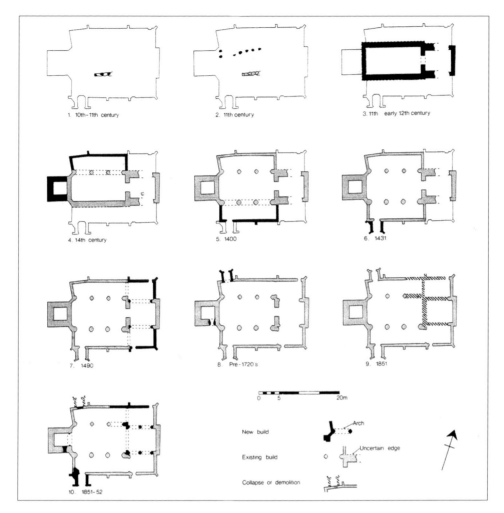

1. 10th-11th century

2. 11th century

3. 11th early 12th century

4. 14th century

5. 1400

6. 1431

7. 1490

8. Pre-1720 s

9. 1851

10. 1851-52

0 5   20m

New build

Existing build

Collapse or demolition

Arch

Uncertain edge

68 Phases of church development, St Martin-at-Palace, from tenth/eleventh centuries to nineteenth century (Hoste Spalding)

of a piece of fifteenth-century chain mail discovered in the roof of the south aisle in 1963. One of the most famous examples of benefaction is the church of St Peter Hungate, where the roof was paid for by Margaret and John Paston; label stops in the south transept may represent them.

Expansion of churches sometimes caused problems within the cramped topography of the medieval city centre. Applications were made on occasion to close lanes, as was done successfully for the Dominican friary in 1345. More frequently, churches were built across thoroughfares as at St John Maddermarket where a passageway pierces the tower or St Gregory where the chancel is built above a lane. A similar situation probably prevailed at the east end of St Peter Mancroft; although here the lane was eventually pushed further to the east and the archway beneath the chancel incorporated as part of a 'processional way' (an undercroft survives below the existing Weavers Lane, immediately east of St Peter Mancroft, perhaps implying a lost building above).

The continual burial of individuals within churchyards led to problems of overspill. The phenomenon, and its topographical effect, was noted by John Evelyn in 1671:

> One thing I observ'd of remarkable in this Citty, that most of the Church-yards (though some of them large enough) were filled up with earth, or rather the congestion of dead bodys on(e) upon another, for want of Earth &c to the very top of the Walls, & many above the wales, so as the Churches seem'd to be built in pitts ...

In theory, overspill could be accommodated from the early fourteenth century by the charnel house established at the cathedral (the Carnary College, now part of the Norwich School, was founded by Bishop Salmon for 'the bones of persons buried in the city of Norwich'). In practice, other solutions were also found. Excavation in 1988 beneath the car park of the Maid's Head Hotel off Palace Street located graves associated with a lost burial chapel. This graveyard and chapel had acted as overspill for the churchyard of SS Simon and Jude since at least 1316 although they were located in the parish of St George Tombland. The site may have been disused by the early fifteenth century.

Churches did not just expand or were rebuilt in the fifteenth century; some continued to be lost, such as that of St Margaret *in combusto*. This parish was

69 Carnary College, Norwich Cathedral (Brian Ayers)

added to that of All Saints Fyebriggate about 1468; St Clement Conesford was added to St Julian in 1482; and St Cuthbert may have disappeared before 1492. It was noted above that elements of the church of St Cuthbert were observed in the 1930s, with burials being recorded in 1952 and 1999 (p.45). Further skeletons were uncovered on the site of St Clement Conesford in 1962 during bulldozing. The church of St Clement itself survived into the eighteenth century, re-used as a barn.

Encroachment upon graveyards was not unknown. The eastern graveyard of St George Tombland was probably cut back in the later Middle Ages as a revival of commercial activity on Tombland led to the establishment of small shops without rear yards on the street frontage (the establishment of St George, probably in the twelfth century, had itself encroached upon Tombland).

Churches could also be associated with industrial activity. A bellfounding pit, together with numbers of bell mould fragments, was excavated to the north of the church of St John the Baptist Timberhill in 1989, within the graveyard. The Timberhill area housed a number of bellfounders in the fifteenth century whose products were marketed throughout Norfolk. The trade was long-lasting and not confined to bells as bellfounders also made other copper alloy goods; waste from sixteenth- or seventeenth century workshops was found within the quarry pits at Ber Street in 1999, not far from St John Timberhill.

Bells were also made within the larger ecclesiastical institutions. A bell-casting pit was found on excavations at the site of the Franciscan friary with the remains of the pedestal of a bell-mould *in situ*. The pit was not the only subterranean feature at the friary: vaulted culverts, probably for the friary water supply although possibly acting as drains, were also discovered. Shallow brick drains channelled water into a main culvert, one such drain utilising a *paramoudra* flint (that is, a flint with a large hole within it) to direct the flow. The main culvert was plotted eastward for a length of some 30m by use of a remote-controlled camera mounted on a small robot tractor.

The predominantly fifteenth-century building campaign at the Dominican friary can be followed in the buildings themselves as purchase of the complex by the city in 1540 has ensured much of their survival. The large preaching nave still stands; with simple piers devoid of ostentatious decoration and an equally simple but soaring hammerbeam roof. The east end of the nave would have been walled off from a central walking space. This wall no longer exists but its footings were observed and recorded during floor repairs in 1993. East of the walking space is the choir with a great decorated east window.

Considerations of space on a marginal riverine site dictated that the cloisters were constructed to the north. The south walk of these is intact, with elements of the east and west walks also surviving. The plan of the north walk has been recovered by excavation, which has also uncovered part of the chapter house, pier shafts of which survive, and the brewhouse.

South of the church was the preaching yard, still an open space. The Dominicans also owned all the property in the angle south-east of the church, formed by the corner of Elm Hill and Princes Street. Buildings here are largely post-medieval but one or two have medieval cellars, one with a lamp niche implying that there may have been friary structures here too. These could have been rented out in order to bring income or been service buildings associated with friary itself; excavation at the Franciscan friary has shown that a new building was erected against the precinct wall on King Street in the fifteenth century, probably as a service range to the kitchen.

Another major building campaign in the later Middle Ages was that at the Great Hospital. Money was given for the west tower in the 1370s; the chapel or choir was completed about 1383, complete with a remarkable roof containing some 252 panels each allegedly decorated with the arms of Anne of Bohemia, wife of Richard II of England; the infirmary nave seems to be an extension of the fifteenth century; and the cloisters were built around 1455 to 1479. The complex included a dining hall and dormitory for the chaplains (monks working in the hospital). To the north was a kitchen and, to the east, a probable chapter house. All of these buildings, except for the kitchen and chapter house, survive.

There was also considerable work at the cathedral in the fifteenth century. Construction of the spire has been mentioned above but this was preceded by other major works. The Erpingham Gate seems to have been constructed in the second quarter of the fifteenth century; it retains much figurative sculpture on

70 Excavation of the Dominican cloisters in 1910/11 (Norfolk & Norwich Archaeological Society)

its voussoirs depicting virgin martyrs, local saints and probably the apostles and is also decorated with the arms of Sir Thomas Erpingham. The Alnwick Gate, providing entry to the palace, was started by Bishop Alnwick but completed by his successor Walter Lyhart who added the doors. Lyhart's rebus (or punning image) of a bishop's mitre above a heart lying on its side is carved on the door to the foot passage. The bishop was clearly fond of such puns; vaults were added to the nave during his episcopate and here a further rebus, this time of a hart (deer) lying down in water, spells out his full name in carvings on several of the nave piers.

The nave vaults are famous for over 250 carved bosses which seek to illustrate a biblical history of the world. These followed in the tradition of fourteenth- and fifteenth-century bosses in the vaults of the cloisters (*colour plate 19*) which depict religious themes. Vaults were added above the presbytery by Bishop Goldwell about 1480. His scheme was different: 94 of 128 bosses consist of the bishop's rebus – a gold well – with 29 of the remainder being of floral design, three bear Goldwell's coat-of-arms and only two are religious. Bishop Nix completed the vaulting of the church with vaults over the transepts early in the sixteenth century. He too had some of the bosses carry his arms but the main scheme tells the New Testament story as far as Christ's ministry.

Away from the cathedral, a further aspect of late medieval religion within Norwich was the provision of anchorages attached to churches for the occupation of solitary hermits or anchorites. Both the Franciscan and Dominican friaries

71 Rebus of Bishop Lyhart on the doors of the Alnwick Gate (Brian Ayers)

Above: 72 The Britons Arms, a possible *beguinage* on Elm Hill (Brian Ayers)

Left: 73 Excavation of fifteenth-century dyehouse in 1972 (Norwich Survey)

provided a cell for an anchorite, remains of that at the Dominican site being visible within the outer face of the north wall of the choir. These remains include a squint through the wall to the high altar. The most famous anchorage in the city was that attached to the church of St Julian which was occupied in the early fifteenth-century by the celebrated mystic, Julian of Norwich, the first woman to write a book in English. The city seems also to have been host to two or three beguinages, women living as religious communities but without vows. One such community may have been housed in the Britons Arms, a fifteenth-century thatched building on Elm Hill.

TRADE AND INDUSTRY

Norwich in the fifteenth century continued to be a major industrial city. Much of this industrial output was directed at the textile trade, although this seems to have suffered a decline relative to its fourteenth-century peak. Dyers and other cloth-finishers nevertheless continued to operate. Excavations on the north side of Westwick Street, at the foot of the medieval *Letestere Row* (a litester was a dyer), in 1972 uncovered a fifteenth-century dyer's workshop. Here, a late thirteenth- or early fourteenth-century building had been adapted for dying with the provision of furnaces, a stoke pit, well and drain. The building remained in use into the sixteenth century.

Artefacts provide further evidence of the textile trade. Wool combs dating from the twelfth to the seventeenth centuries have been recovered. Tenter hooks are also known, used when dyed cloth was stretched on tenting frames; the earliest example is fifteenth-century in date. An iron harbick, used to secure cloth to the cropping board during shearing, was found at a site on Oak Street. The textile trade was also developing; 'dornix', a type of cloth used for wall hangings and bed coverings, was supplementing worsted as a significant product.

Objects recovered from excavations point to a range of trades and industries. Fifteenth-century ironworking and woodworking tools, leatherworkers' equipment, boneworking rough-outs, whetstones and balance pans have all been recorded. Bone parchment prickers and pens made from the radius of a goose have also been found. Industrial activity can, of course, be determined from waste; excavation in 1999 recorded massive dumping of ironworking waste off Oak Street as part of riverside land reclamation.

In addition, the city was developing its specialised industries, Norwich painted glass being particularly important in the fifteenth century. Great quantities of this were removed from the friaries in the sixteenth century or smashed in churches in the seventeenth century but good examples still survive, notably in the east window of St Peter Mancroft (where one of the panels depicts the fifteenth-century cloth merchant Robert Toppes and his wife, the man who probably built Dragon Hall, above p.118) and in the Guildhall (*colour plate 23*). Other glass has been located on excavations. Painted window glass discovered at the Franciscan friary seems to have come from a window depicting the Crucifixion. A hoard of painted figurative glass was discovered on King Street in 2000, possibly from the church of St Peter Parmentergate. In 2002, glass excavated at the site of the Carmelite friary may have been associated with a documented window given by John of Gaunt (*colour plate 18*).

It is likely that the production of works of art to adorn churches and the houses of the merchant class was also undertaken in Norwich. As a rare surviving example, the Despencer retable at the cathedral is almost certainly of local craftsmanship. A remarkable fourteenth-century discovery was made at the Franciscan friary excavation in the form of an oyster shell painter's palette – complete with traces of the pigments vermilion (red), azurite (blue) and calcium carbonate (white) – suggesting the painting of walls or statues within the church (*colour plate 12*). Subsequently two further such objects have been found – at the Millennium Library site (where the palette contained a red pigment) and at the cathedral (green pigment).

Commercially the market suffered in the aftermath of the plague but recovered in the late fourteenth century. Finds of pottery and other artefacts testify to the city's trade contacts in the later Middle Ages. As examples, two complete Spanish vessels together with fifteenth-century Italian majolica were found at All Saints Green in 1970. The commercial importance of the river continued to be recognised, although many goods were shipped by barge from Great Yarmouth where most maritime trade was now centred. The construction of Dragon Hall, almost certainly to facilitate the sale of cloth, took place at the waterfront where transhipment was easiest. The provision of a covered passageway beneath the wide rear arcade of Dragon Hall parallels the covered arcades of warehouses at King's Lynn and other ports, enabling goods to be sheltered quickly.

Clerics as well as merchants sought such frontages; the Abbot of Wendling in central Norfolk had a staith at Abbey Lane which he leased to the city but where he maintained a brewery, presumably using water from the river. Other houses with a riverside location included Binham. Bromholm, Chicksand, Ely, Hickling and Sawteries (Sawtry, Hampshire). The practice had been long-established – the abbey of Woburn, for instance, had a stone house on the Dragon Hall site in the thirteenth century but seems to have sold it by 1351/2 at the latest.

The existence of such buildings emphasises the importance of Norwich as both an administrative and as a trading centre. At least 42 ecclesiastical institutions had houses in Norwich to administer their trade and provide hostels for their staff. The Cistercian monasteries of Vaudey (Lincolnshire), Pipewell (Northamptonshire), Merivale and Combe (Warwickshire), Warden

(Bedfordshire) and Garendon (Leicestershire) all had property in the city. Traces of such buildings occasionally survive or are recovered by excavation. Elements of the city house of the Priory of Augustinian Canons at Ixworth in Suffolk still stand on Colegate. The Abbot of Waltham maintained a property on Fishergate, part of which was excavated in 1985. The city house of the Abbey of North Creake (near Burnham Market in north-west Norfolk) was excavated in 1978 on the corner of St Martin's Lane and Oak Street.

This excavation was the most comprehensive to date on such a building of a religious institution in Norwich. The abbey seems to have acquired the property and built a house about 1332. Creake was a poor foundation and the first building was a mean two-roomed structure of clay walls, although with two hearths, set back from the Oak Street frontage. It was rebuilt as a two-roomed range up to the frontage in the fifteenth century with brick and flint rubble walls and a range of three rooms behind it. Two of these rooms were clay-walled, implying that they were single storey in contrast to the street frontage range. Two ovens in one of the rooms suggest that the building was a kitchen or bakehouse.

The rural gentry also owned property in the city. The Paston family are the most famous example, owning houses on Elm Hill and King Street, but other famous names included those of Berney, Coke, Heydon and Hobart. Sir Thomas Erpingham had a large house off World's End Lane at the beginning of the fifteenth century. Substantial parts of this survived until 1858 when it was demolished to make way for a gasworks. Its construction had entailed encroachment upon the river by some 25ft and it was furnished with a tower. Destruction by the gasworks was thorough, however, and nothing remained for archaeological recording when the site was observed during a watching brief in 1985.

Norwich at the end of the fifteenth century was therefore an affluent city with major secular and ecclesiastical buildings and institutions, a diverse economic base and a regional importance. The evidence for its material culture comes from both surviving buildings and, increasingly, from archaeological excavations. The size and diversity of property throughout the city, and the evidence for the social organisation and economic commitment needed to enable Norwich to function effectively, illustrate a city able to adapt to both political problems and pandemic disaster. The sixteenth century was to bring even greater change, starting with two further disasters in one year, the *annus horribilis* of 1507.

7

THE POST-MEDIEVAL CITY

At the beginning of the sixteenth century, the Almoner of Norwich Cathedral Priory was in difficulty with his accounts. Rents, formerly £10 a year, had fallen to only 19s 4d. The reasons given for this were 'the great fires', the evidence for which was summarised by Blomefield in the eighteenth century: 'on the 25th day of April [modern scholarship has re-dated this to March] 1507 a fire broke out, which burnt with continual violence four days …', followed in June the same year by 'another lamentable fire, which burnt two days and a night'. Blomefield calculated that some 718 houses with most of their goods were burnt in 16 parishes.

The fires were clearly devastating and affected some of the most affluent as well as impoverished parts of the city. They were not the sole reason for the Almoner's difficulties, however; rents had been declining for some years but the drop in 1507 was certainly dramatic. The disaster, therefore, added to the economic problems of early sixteenth-century Norwich but was not the cause of them.

It is unclear how the city responded to this crisis, other than by a measure enacted in 1509 to ensure that buildings were to be covered in tile rather than reed. Probably some 40 per cent of the housing stock had been destroyed, inevitably placing considerable pressure on the surviving structures. Archaeological evidence, particularly from the 1976 excavations at Alms Lane, suggests that, while there was some new building with flint and brick walled structures, in general the exploitation of the site was intensified with the infilling of yards and the expansion of existing buildings.

This evidence complements work elsewhere which indicates that not all the sites devastated by fire were rebuilt immediately. Buildings destroyed on the corner of Pottergate and St Laurence's Lane were not replaced until the seventeenth century. This was not atypical; the City considered the situation so bad in 1534 that it sought to compel rebuilding or enclosure of land with a wall. As late as 1570 the City Assembly could record that, resulting from fire, 'many goodly buyldinges and howses are becom gardens and orteyards wheare somtyme enhabited artificers and others …'.

It has been suggested, nevertheless, that the 'great rebuilding', noted elsewhere in later sixteenth-century England, may have begun a generation or more earlier

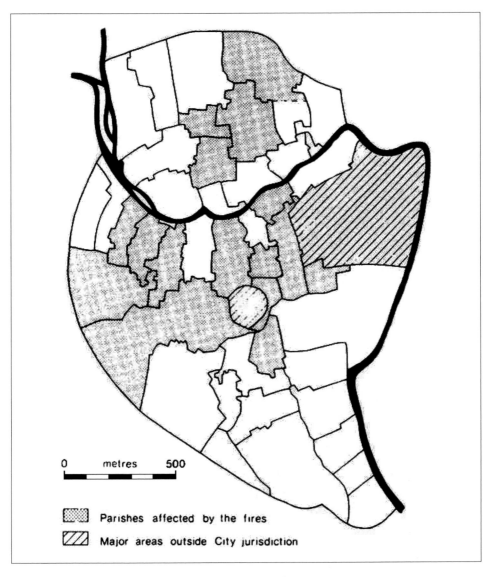

74 Plan of parishes affected by fires in 1507 (Norwich Survey)

in Norwich, in part due to the perforce circumstances induced by the fires (*colour plate 26*). There is some cartographic evidence to support this idea; the 'Sanctuary Plan' of 1541 is the earliest-known map of the city and, although crude, illustrates some 70 or so houses. Nearly all of these have a chimney implying a degree of sophistication across the city, perhaps inspired by fire-control measures introduced following the 1507 disaster.

It therefore remains difficult to clarify the situation concerning the housing stock of the early sixteenth century. Further excavation will help as will examination of surviving buildings. Although only some 214 medieval and post-medieval buildings predating 1700 are known to be still standing, it is likely that about 200 of these date to the sixteenth and seventeenth centuries. It is probable that different development chronologies will be discovered for different parts of the city, reflecting social and economic factors as much as recovery from fire devastation.

Recovery was not helped by a general economic malaise in the city at the beginning of the sixteenth century. Worsted exports in particular were suffering and protectionist legislation and regulation did little to revive this moribund industry. The malaise dragged on into the mid century; weeds were growing in the market place in 1544 and, in the previous year, a herd of cows interrupted a service in the neighbouring church of St Peter Mancroft.

There was, nevertheless, still wealth in Norwich and ostentatious displays to indicate this survive. The great of the city were still building, either houses as at Bacon House on Colegate where the spectacular street frontage dates in part from the 1530s, or in donations to churches – the Thorp chapel of St Michael Coslany (*colour plate 20*) was constructed about 1500 with an impressive display of flushwork decoration. The wealthy merchant Robert Jannys had a terracotta tomb made for the church of St George Colegate in 1530 (either by

75 Council Chamber in the Guildhall (Brian Ayers)

the same craftsman who made the famous Bedingfeld tombs at Oxborough or using the same moulds) while, slightly more modestly, Philip Curson left money in 1506 to pave the chancel of St Peter Mancroft in marble.

The ostentation spilt over into public buildings. A Market Cross some 60-70ft (20m) high, standing on a plinth 30ft (9m) wide, was built at the expense of John Rightwise in 1501/03. It contained a chapel although in later years this was used as a grain store. Demolished in 1732, its footings were probably those uncovered in 1909 and described as 'massive remains'. Probably damaged in market refurbishment in the 1930s, these foundations were exposed again when new market stalls were laid out in 2005. The octagonal base of the Market Cross can now be traced, marked out in the paving between the modern market stalls.

A grand Council Chamber was erected within the Guildhall in the 1530s, its roof with moulded tie-beams and ornamental pendants and, beneath, contemporary oak panelling with posts carved with animal heads. These were the endowments of rich men who helped to make Norwich the highest taxed provincial city in the 1520s but whose expenditure and public profile masked a much larger underclass of urban poor and relatively impoverished artisans.

THE REFORMATION

The Reformation necessarily brought considerable disruption to the city. Much of Norwich and its surrounding area was dominated by the great monastic institutions, notably those of the cathedral priory and the priory of Carrow. Large parts of the city were given over to monastic precincts and there were numerous hospitals, chantries, anchorages and a school. Removal of these in the 1530s and 1540s severely disrupted the local economy but also released much land for development.

An example of rapid exploitation of the new circumstances is that undertaken by Thomas Howard, the third Duke of Norfolk. He was granted 'the site, church, house, bells, fisheries, yards, buildings and all possessions' of the Franciscan friary in Norwich in 1539. While he did not immediately clear the site (the 'great house' of the friary, probably the living quarters of the friars, was pulled down in 1565/66 at the charge of the city), he certainly began to ransack the structures. Repairs about 1540 to the Blackfriars were assisted by '17 loads of paving tile brought from the Grey-friars' while a new buttery and pantry were built 'with spars of the Grey Friars chancel roof'.

Demolition of the Franciscan friary was thorough. Excavations on the site in 1993 found few walls surviving above foundation level and nearly all freestone gone. Great dumps of waste material consisted entirely of mortar and small fragments of flint; all other material had been removed. Floor tiles had been lifted (possibly for the repairs at the Blackfriars) and marble was also taken although two marble floor slabs were overlooked and survived to be recorded.

Other sites were probably also cleared. A ruined wall and arch are depicted on Cuningham's plan of 1558 on the site of the Carmelite friary but the church had gone. The site of the Norman Hospital is shown as open space although buildings are known to have been standing in 1571. The Augustinian friary was demolished and eventually became a celebrated garden. The old Blackfriars site off Colegate was open land in 1558.

Some monastic structures were re-used, those of the Dominicans being the most outstanding examples. The Carnary College was acquired for use as a grammar school (replacing the dissolved monastic school), thus ensuring its survival. The Great Hospital was re-founded with a new constitution so it too survived. A further outstanding survival is that of the early sixteenth-century prioress's wing at Carrow, outside the city walls. This was built by Isabelle Wygun (her rebus of the letter 'y' with a cannon or gun is extant in a spandrel of a doorway in the west wall) and was converted in the eighteenth century into a house. It now forms part of the staff facilities for Colman's factory. Within the city, the large chapel of St Mary-in-the Fields was demolished but the collegiate buildings were converted into a house which, in the 1750s, was remodelled as an Assembly House. Fire swept the central range in 1995, enabling recording of the fabric, nearly all of which related to the remodelling.

Churches were also lost or went out of use at or shortly after the time of the Reformation. Losses were the churches of All Saints Fyebriggate which was gone by 1551; St Bartholomew on Ber Street (by 1550); St Botolph (by 1548); St Crowche (by 1551); St Martin in Balliva (about 1558); St Mary in the Marsh (about 1564); St Mary Unbrent (about 1540); and St Olave (1546). The church of St Mary the Less was added to St George Tombland in 1542 but the building still stands.

With minor exceptions, there is no surviving visible evidence of the lost churches. Elements of some of them continue, nevertheless, to influence the modern urban topography or exist within later structures. It seems likely that All Saints was sold, the nave passing to one purchaser and the chancel to another. The site of the nave was developed as a Co-op store with a fine terracotta façade in the 1930s; this has now been converted into a health centre and the site of the chancel, previously waste ground, re-united with it (after 450 years) as the centre's car park. St Bartholomew was still standing in the 1930s when its interior was photographed in use as a store; it was bombed in the Second World War and only one corner of the west end now survives.

The site of St Botolph was destroyed without record for the Anglia Square development in 1974 but anonymous information recounts the numerous skeletons uncovered at the time. The site of St Martin in Balliva was also destroyed with little record in 1970 although skeletons were found together with quantities of pins, perhaps implying burial in shrouds. Parts of the church and graveyard may yet survive and a stone coffin, uncovered in road works in 1910, was probably from the site.

The city was the centre of activity during Kett's Rebellion of 1549 when it was besieged by an army of rebels estimated at 30,000. The rebels established headquarters buildings on the edge of Mousehold Heath in the recently-dissolved St Leonard's Priory and St Michael's Chapel (the remains of the latter are still known as 'Kett's Castle'). The attack on the city led to partial destruction of the Cow Tower where the battlements were hit by cannon fire. The rebels took the city from the east but were in turn forced out by royal forces under the Earl of Warwick. He breached the western walls and other damage included the firing of houses, the demolition of Whitefriars Bridge and burning of buildings at the Common Staith and the Great Hospital. Traces of burning still exist at the top of the Cow Tower.

While Norwich thus had both economic and political problems during the first half of the sixteenth century, it remained nevertheless a city of the first rank. It had achieved this without any major contribution by the noblest families of the land and, indeed, direct royal and aristocratic influence in Norwich is notable for its absence through much of the later medieval period.

Attempts to obtain such influence were made in the sixteenth century. The Earl of Surrey built a house on Surrey Street before 1513 (it survived into the nineteenth century) with a successor Earl eventually acquiring the site of the Augustinian friary and erecting a fine seventeenth-century house there. The Duke of Norfolk, however, determined to build a palace in Norwich and this was erected between 1561 and 1567. The site chosen was hardly propitious; anxious to be close to the centre of a populous city, the Duke acquired the only place available, next to the river downstream of the dyers. A visitor in 1681 (shortly after refurbishment of the building) described it as a 'sumptuous new-built house, not yet finished within, but seated in a dung-hole place ...'. It was never a popular residence.

Excavations in 1974 (the palace was abandoned before 1711 and most buildings destroyed by 1806 although the bowling alley survived into the twentieth century and was photographed) revealed that enormous quantities of soil had been brought in to level up the site prior to building. Massive brick foundations were inserted but none of these reached bedrock (the infill overlies a gravel terrace) and cracking of the walls occurred. A staircase tower, probably part of the kitchens, and outbuildings were discovered. There was considerable evidence of the re-use of materials, probably from ecclesiastical sites in the city, but also from further afield; a memorial slab was found on the site in 1849 from the Abbey of St Benet at Holme, east of Norwich on the river Bure.

THE 'STRANGERS'

The Duke of Norfolk was not the only 'incomer' to the city in the sixteenth century. In 1565, the city authorities invited 'Dutch' cloth manufacturers to settle in the city. Initially the invitation extended to 24 Dutch and six Walloon master weavers but numbers increased rapidly so that by 1579 there were about 6000 'Strangers' in the city. Plague in that year killed disproportionately large numbers of these immigrants, probably as a result of cramped living conditions, but by the early seventeenth century it is probable that they constituted one third of the population.

The social impact must have been great (and occasional movements to expel them are known) but their economic importance was even greater. The Strangers effectively revitalised the stagnant Norwich cloth trade, introducing new techniques and fabrics and laying the basis for the extraordinary wealth of the city in the seventeenth and early eighteenth centuries.

The Strangers left their mark on the city. The church of St Mary the Less, 'the French church', probably survives because it was used by the Walloons. The choir of the Dominican friary, now known as Blackfriars Hall, was the Dutch church and an annual service in Dutch continued to be held until early in the twentieth century. A great number of the Strangers settled initially on the north bank of the river Wensum, in parishes such as that of St George Colegate or St Michael Coslany. Documentary research has uncovered surnames of individuals and family groups such as Ceuleman, De Clerke, Dierick, Fromanteels, Moenes and Vancuelen while a late sixteenth memorial stone survives within St Michael's to 'Hubertus van Ypres'.

Excavations on the north bank, both at Alms Lane in 1976 and, a little further to the north, at Calvert Street in 1989/90, recovered evidence of probable Dutch communities. Finds included dress fittings, hair ornaments and clay pipes of Dutch type or manufacture. An eighteenth-century structure at Alms Lane, with a base for a copper, was interpreted as a wash-house, perhaps for scouring yarn. A Walloon weaver, Jacob Votier, was a tenant on the site in 1725. Low Countries pottery was common from both excavations although this need not necessarily reflect Dutch occupation. Many sites in Norwich contain fragments of such vessels which were clearly in widespread use from the later medieval period. Some vessel types, however, might suggest the distinctive cooking habits of an immigrant community; frying pans or skillets seem to have been introduced by Dutch settlers as early as the fifteenth century.

The Strangers were also active in areas other than textiles, working as goldsmiths or builders and printers. Two refugees from Antwerp, Jasper Andries and Jacob Janson, established the first kiln in England for the production of tin-glazed pottery on Ber Street in 1567. Recent excavation on the site failed to locate the kiln which may have been destroyed by a large and deep cellar but waster sherds have been found.

Right: 76 Seventeenth-century redware skillet from Botolph Street (Norfolk Museums & Archaeology Service)

Below: 77 Werra ware plate (Hoste Spalding)

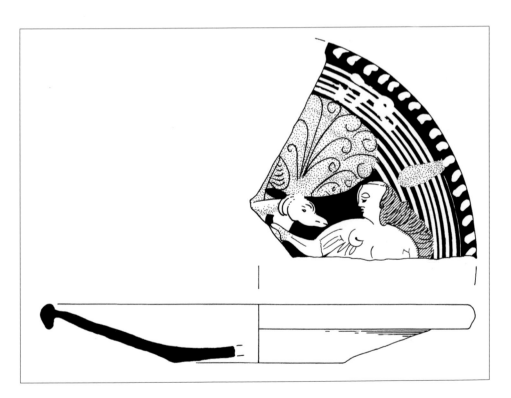

The revitalisation of the cloth industry was accompanied by a revolution in the manner of textile production in the city. The medieval cloth trade, although centred on Norwich, was essentially one of rural manufacture and urban cloth finishing and distribution. By the late sixteenth and seventeenth centuries this had changed with manufacture becoming an important part of the urban process. Much of the cloth was woven by small groups of weavers, working to a master weaver. This meant that production was distributed throughout the city, weavers working in their own homes. The practice was memorably, if perhaps somewhat fancifully, summarised by Daniel Defoe when he visited Norwich in the 1720s:

> if a stranger was only to ride thro' or view the city of Norwich for a day he would have much ... reason to think that it was a town without inhabitants ... the case is this; the inhabitants being all busie at their manufactures, dwell in their garrets at their looms, and in their combing-shops, so they call them, twisting mills, and other work-houses ...

The exaggeration may not be that far from the mark; twenty years earlier Celia Fiennes had noted that the inhabitants were 'all employ'd in spinning knitting weaveing dying scouring fulling or bleaching their stuffs ...'.

Production of cloth certainly did take place in 'garrets' and it is likely that many of the distinctive dormer windows which still grace a great number of Norwich buildings were built to allow light into such workshops. It is apparent from recent research, however, that such use of garret rooms was only one activity among many. Examination of inventories for the period 1580 to 1730 (some 871 in all) revealed that the percentage of garrets used for working never exceeded 31 (and that as late as 1705-30) while the percentage for sleeping never fell below 53 (1630-54).

BUILDINGS AND URBAN DEVELOPMENT

This work on inventories complements study of extant buildings and archaeological excavation. The development of houses and house use in post-medieval Norwich is one which has been but little studied save for the very recent work by Chris King on the élite houses. The 1976 Alms Lane site remains the best example of an intensively sampled urban landscape although it also clear from other sites, such as from excavation at Whitefriars in 1992 or survey at Dragon Hall, that the sixteenth and seventeenth centuries were periods when earlier structures were being divided up to provide accommodation (a process that may have started in the fifteenth century at Dragon Hall). The inventories, however, many of which relate to parishes north of the river and therefore, while not to poor houses, generally to the middling affluent rather than the rich, enable the development of such features as heated rooms or wash-houses to be charted.

The housing situation is of importance because, not withstanding Stranger immigration, the proportion of the East Anglian population living in towns changed significantly during the sixteenth and seventeenth centuries. Population probably grew by half between the 1520s and 1670 but the proportion of the Norfolk population living in Norwich doubled in the same period. The economic and social importance of Norwich was therefore heightened but the extra people had to have somewhere to live.

It is indicative of the extraordinary size of Norwich and the way in which existing developed land was utilised more rigorously (no doubt encouraged in part by a landlord desire to maximise profits) that the city absorbed the increase in population without significant encroachment on the considerable open space within the walls or by suburban development. The city was indeed notable for its lack of suburbs. Heigham Street, to the west, was a small medieval suburb essentially created when it was left outside the medieval city wall. Its church of St Bartholomew was bombed in 1942 and only the tower still stands. A sixteenth-century timber-framed building – now the Gibraltar Gardens public house – escaped the bombing but a fine house with a sixteenth-century gable and a main façade of 1615 called the Dolphin Inn did not. This building housed Bishop Hall during the Interregnum in the 1640s and 1650s. It has been rebuilt since the war but only the façade remains of the original house.

An impoverished suburb was probably established outside the Pockthorpe Gate to the east of the city by the sixteenth century. It was noted above that crop processing and hornworking took place in this area in the thirteenth and fourteenth centuries, presumably associated with buildings. William Cuningham's plan of 1558 shows houses along both sides of the road outside the gate with further buildings running up part of what is now Silver Road. The area did not develop however; Cole's plan of 1807 shows the extent of occupation as little more than that in the sixteenth century.

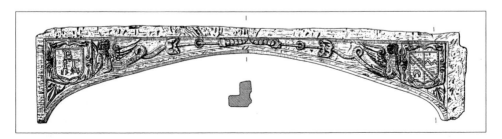

78 Decorated timber door-head of 1594 from Dragon Hall (NAU Archaeology)

The only other suburban development prior to the late eighteenth century was on Bracondale to the south. Here the 'Manor House' was built at the beginning of the seventeenth century and, in the same location, a Jacobean garden tower from the roof of which were commanding views of the Wensum and Yare valleys. Both survive. They are of brick, the manor house with characteristically 'Dutch' gables, the tower with brick-mullioned windows and doors. Other houses followed in the later seventeenth and eighteenth centuries.

The later sixteenth century saw a revitalisation of public works. Whitefriars Bridge was rebuilt in 1590 while in 1583 John Foster and Alexander Peele, citizens and plumbers of London,

> erected buyled and sette up at or nere New Mylles, a mylle with all things thereto belongeng to dryve and conveighe water by and throughe certaine pypes of lead lyeng and beeyng in dyvers streets and churchyardes to the Market Cross ...

A 'systern' was established at the Cross with another on Tombland although no trace of either has been recorded. Post-medieval waterpipes were observed nearby on St Faith's Lane in 1972 and three intact examples were recovered from excavations on the site of the Greyfriars precinct in 1993.

The supply of water was also the function of an ornate conduit erected by Robert Gybson, a wealthy beer brewer, in 1577. This stands on Westwick Street (re-erected in a reversed position to protect it from traffic) and was built to provide public access to water from a well which previously had been approached via a lane. Gybson was given consent to close the lane provided that 'at his proper costs and charges in a conduit or cock of lead [he] bring the water ... up into the street for the case of the common people ...'.

THE CIVIL WAR AND AFTER

Norwich was loyal to Parliament during the Civil War and remote from the fighting. There were alterations, nevertheless, to the urban fabric. The gates to the city were strengthened by rampiring and gun emplacements were established on the castle mound. An arsenal was created in the Committee House; this blew up during a riot in 1648 (the 'Great Blow'), killing many and destroying much glass in St Peter Mancroft Church. The cathedral was desecrated, the evicted Bishop Hall describing the scene:

> What clattering of glasses! What beating down of walls! What tearing up of monuments! What pulling down of seats! What wresting out of iron and brass from the windows and graves! What defacing of arms! What demolishing of curious

stonework, that had not any representation in the world, but only the cost of the founder, and skill of the mason!

The cathedral was spared the fate urged on Parliament by the citizens of Great Yarmouth who petitioned for its destruction so that the materials 'of that vast and altogether useless Cathedral in Norwich' could be used 'towards the building of a work house to employ our almost starved poor and repairing our piers ...'. Archaeological evidence survives, nevertheless, for the violence done to the building; a piece of lead shot embedded in the monument to Bishop Goldwell is almost certainly a relic of the Civil War.

The seventeenth century increasingly brought greater change to Norwich even if the Civil War did not. Study of the surviving building stock has shown that many single-celled buildings were erected (such as the house of William Watson on St George's Street where a single cell unit was attached to a timber-framed building to create a two- or three-cell block) while it is clear from an early eighteenth-century painting of the city that it now contained many substantial houses. The large map of Cleer, published in 1696, does not depict these, showing the built-up areas as blocks of property, but the Corbridge map of 1727

79 William Watson's house, St George's Street (Brian Ayers)

is more detailed, decorating its border with the greater houses of the day, while the Norwich antiquarian John Kirkpatrick frequently sketched buildings.

Many of these were probably built in the traditional timber-framed manner but also utilising flint and brick such as 56-60 King Street. These houses, with a flourish of curvilinear gables, are characteristic of many of the now lost seventeenth-century buildings of Norwich. Other good examples of buildings of the period survive on Colegate. The growth of population will have led inevitably to social problems such as that of rubbish disposal. Some form of rubbish collection is recorded as early as 1518 and it was noted at Alms Lane that rubbish disposal on site had effectively ceased by the end of the seventeenth century. Quantities of material were certainly being thrown into the river margins, as evidenced at the Duke's Palace site, to level the riparian land. Such levelling has also been observed on the lower parts of the Greyfriars site, in excavations in the Lower Close and at the castle where vast amounts of rubbish were used to fill the great ditches.

Such movement of large quantities of refuse is likely to have been common; there is a growing body of evidence to suggest that much of the minor 'hilliness'

80 Drawing by John Kirkpatrick of the Castle Bridge (Norfolk Museums & Archaeology Service)

of Norwich was levelled out by the eighteenth century. The cockeys or streams which were utilised for much of the medieval period tend to disappear from the records although some, such as the Great Cockey, are known to have been culverted. The small stream valleys also disappeared, as observed on St George's Street in 1986 or at the Royal Arcade in 1988 where the deeper part of the cockey valley was seen to be infilled by up to 4m of material. Levelling in both these instances probably dated from the medieval period but the lessening of slopes, such as that from the river up Rose Lane, continued in later centuries.

TRADE, INDUSTRY AND SOCIETY

A further consequence of the increase in population was an increase in the importance of Norwich as a regional centre, particularly as a market. The range of market activities astounded Thomas Baskerville when he visited in 1681:

> ... the chief market-place of this city ... vastly full of provisions ... where I saw the greatest shambles for butchers' meat I had ever yet seen, and the like also for poultry and dairy meats, which dairy people also bring many quarters of veal with their butter and cheese, and I believe also in their seasons pork and hog-meats ... and such kind of people as sell fish ... viz. crabs, flounders, mackerel, very cheap, but lobster for sea fish and pike or jack for river fish were dear enough. They asked me for one pike under 2 foot, 2s 6d, and for a pot of pickled oysters they would have a shilling. Here I saw excellent oatmeal which being curiously hulled looked like French barley, with great store of gingerbread and other edible things. And for grain in the corn market ... I saw wheat, rye, oats, malt ground and not ground, French wheat, and but little barley, because the season for malting was over ...

Much of this trade may also be discernible in the archaeological record although, to date, few well-preserved post-medieval contexts have been sampled for environmental analysis. More tangible evidence for the importance of Norwich, and for the high quality and variety of material brought into the city, can be observed in artefacts recovered from excavations or watching briefs. At the Castle Mall site, sixteenth- and seventeenth-century material included a decorated German powder horn, a Palissy Ware dish from south-western France with an enamel depiction of St John the Evangelist (*colour plate 25*), a decorated head dress ornament from the Low Countries, ornate Dutch slipwares and, more prosaically, a German bird whistle.

Excavation of a well in St Stephen's Street in 1976 produced a particularly fine range of imported and local ceramics. The imports, both English and continental and which could be phased into four phases spanning the seventeenth century,

81 Sixteenth-century powder horn
(Hoste Spalding)

consisted of Weser Slipware, Surrey White Ware, Metropolitan Slipware, Frechen Stoneware, Dutch and English Tin-glazed Earthenwares, a fragment of Hispano-Moresque Luste Ware bowl, Italian Marble Ware, Dutch Slipware, Staffordshire Combed Slipware and Westerwald Stoneware. The assemblage was atypical in that it was securely stratified but was typical of the range of material recovered on sites across the city. Occasionally more exotic imports are located such as a Chinese soapstone seal which was recovered from the city ditch.

Exports from Norwich were dominated by textiles; pattern books survive from the early eighteenth century with examples of Norwich worsteds, half-silks and callimancoes carefully inserted into the pages. The textile trade was of supreme importance to post-medieval Norwich. It eclipsed all other economic activity between 1660 and 1730 and was fiercely defended by the city authorities. A Weavers Company was formed in 1650 and this supervised much of the output (a wooden plaque, over six feet high and bearing the Weavers' Arms, survives in the Bridewell Museum). Many company seals, which were originally attached to the cloth, have been found, notably in London, the main export market although recently three important assemblages have been recovered from Norwich (from the Franciscan friary site in 1993, Fishergate in 1999 and Palace Street in 2000).

The friary site seals date from the sixteenth to eighteenth centuries and relate to both local products, such as worsteds, and to imports – one seal comes from Augsburg noted for its fustians and another from Strasbourg which produced serges, bays, says and tapestries. The finds from Fishergate date to the sixteenth and seventeenth centuries and appear to be all local, ranging from relatively coarse to fine fabrics. One seal is from the Norwich Russel Company, dating from the mid sixteenth to the seventeenth centuries, russel being a woollen fabric. Another seal bears a ship design, emblematic of the Walloon community and thus associated with the 'New Draperies'. The Palace Street seals also date from the sixteenth and seventeenth centuries.

By the eighteenth century the textile trade had created a number of affluent merchants and these left their mark on the city in the houses which they erected for themselves, some of which still stand. Two fine such buildings are on Colegate, built by the Harvey family. No. 18 Colegate belonged to Robert Harvey who was mayor in 1748. It has a splendid door on to the street but originally had an equally splendid one to the river, emphasising the continuing importance of the Wensum. Next door, at No. 20 is the house of Robert Harvey which incorporates a seventeenth-century range at the rear facing the river and contains good eighteenth-century plasterwork. Across the road stands No 3 Colegate, built for the Ives family. The Harveys and Ives inter-married, their parish church of St Clement containing memorials to both families.

Other grand eighteenth-century buildings stand south of the river too. Alderman Thomas Churchman's house was originally built by 1727 but it was partly demolished by his son who constructed the grand front now visible on Upper St Giles Street. It contains exceptionally rich plasterwork and wall paintings. John Patteson built a fine house on Surrey Street in 1764. It now forms offices for the Norwich Union, insurance and banking being two further developments within the city's economy in the1700s. The Gurney family, which had acted successfully as yarn merchants, created Gurneys Bank in 1775.

More traditional industries such as leatherworking, hornworking and tanning remained important in post-medieval Norwich. Evidence for the latter two activities has been located outside the walls on Heigham Street in 1994. Traditional quarrying of the chalk hillsides was probably supplemented with mining for flint. Extensive galleries are now known in parts of Norwich, notably beneath Ber Street, off Rosary Road to the east of the walled city, and beneath the Earlham Road to the west. These galleries are difficult to date, although it is currently thought unlikely that they precede the sixteenth century, exploitation

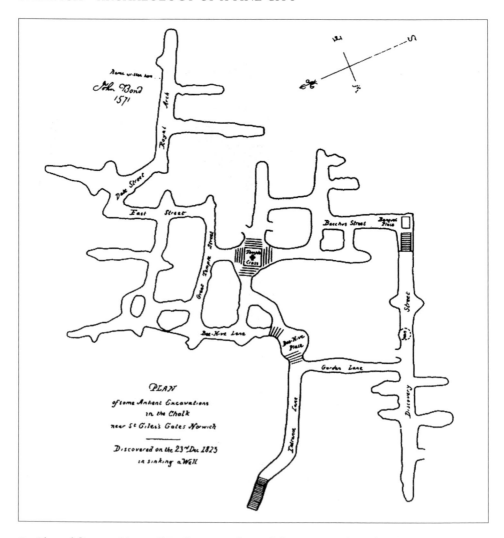

82 Plan of flint workings off Earlham Road (Norfolk & Norwich Archaeological Society)

continuing into the nineteenth century. Subsidence continues to be a problem when workings collapse. A previously unknown gallery was observed in 1988 after a bus sank into the Earlham Road. The working was little higher than the seam of flint (some 2ft) with pick marks visible in the chalk.

Other new industries were created of which an important one for common traces in archaeological deposits is that of clay pipemaking. This began in the seventeenth century and fragments of discarded pipekiln have been discovered in post-medieval ditch fills at the castle. Furniture from pipekilns has been recovered from a site on Pottergate, next to the nineteenth-century 'Pipeburners Yard'.

The developing society of Norwich led to a considerable amount of civic building in the later seventeenth and eighteenth centuries. Nonconformity was

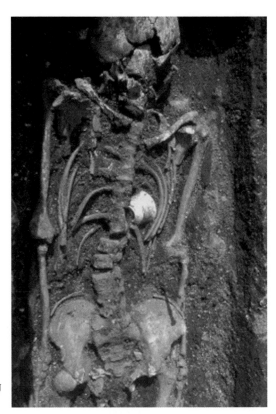

83 Anabaptist burial with teacup (NAU Archaeology)

an important movement in the city. This has been seen recently in excavation when part of an Anabaptist graveyard was uncovered on the site of the Carmelite friary in 2002 (*colour plate 29*). More obviously, a fine early chapel still stands on Colegate: the Old Meeting House (Congregational) of 1693. Construction of this building was made possible after the Act of Toleration of 1689 but it is nevertheless set well back from the street frontage. Its design, however, is less modest than its location, four exceptionally large Corinthian capitals dominating the façade above brick pilasters. The yard is paved with imported Dutch bricks, stressing the link of the church with the Netherlands, a link which persisted throughout the eighteenth century as testified by a ledger slab inscribed in 1794 to Thomas Browne, 'late of Rotterdam'.

Another seventeenth-century chapel which does not survive is that of the Quakers, built on part of Gildencroft in 1699. This was bombed in 1942 but the adjacent burial ground, for which licence was gained in 1690, remains. The grand Octagon Chapel (Presbyterian, now Unitarian) was built on Colegate in 1756 by Thomas Ivory (*colour plate 28*). Its design impressed John Wesley who described it as 'the most elegant meeting house in Europe' although he went on to wonder 'how shall the old coarse Gospel … find admission here'?

Recently, the large building facing the Market Place between Dove Street and Exchange Street has been identified as the probable Goldsmiths' Hall, occupying a site owned by the goldsmiths since the thirteenth century and rebuilt about 1700. The first-floor hall, with nine bays, the central one of which has a door, is likely to have formed a grandstand view for the goldsmiths on festive occasions when the space immediately in front of the east face of the Guildhall would be used for processions and other events. The Master of the Goldsmiths could stand in the first-floor doorway with his Brethren in the windows to either side (*colour plate 27*).

The earliest purpose-built mental hospital, the Bethel Hospital, was founded in Norwich in 1724, using a house of 1712/13. It still contains its original boardroom. Later in the century, the Norfolk & Norwich Hospital was founded outside St Stephen's Gate, the first buildings being erected in 1770-5. Other public works including significant repairs on the city defences in 1727(primarily the Queen's Road stretch, now almost entirely lost above ground) and to the levelling of the castle earthworks south of the mound for a cattle market in 1738. This last has recently been investigated in the Castle Mall excavations where it was also clear that systematic exploitation of the castle area for sands and gravels had preceded levelling.

Other public, or at least semi-public, spaces were gardens and orchards. Norwich was famous for these with Corbridge's plan of 1727 detailing many,

84 Norwich Castle by Samuel and Nathaniel Buck, 1738 (Norfolk Museums & Archaeology Service)

particularly in the eastern part of the walled city. Much of the Greyfriars site was given over to such gardens and part of a garden and a probable path were excavated here in 1993. The Earl of Surrey developed the Augustinian friary site as gardens and these were visited by Thomas Baskerville in 1681. He arrived by boat where

> the boatman brought us to a fair garden ... having handsome stairs leading to the water by which we ascended into the garden and saw a good bowling-green, and many fine walks; the gardener now keeping good liquors and fruits to entertain such as come to see it.

All trace of this garden was destroyed by development in 1970. Smaller private gardens were also worthy of note; John Evelyn wrote of 'the flower-gardens, which all the inhabitants excell in of this Citty ...'. Evelyn visited in 1671 and was taken by his host, Sir Thomas Browne, to Browne's famous herb garden which he maintained near the Haymarket in the heart of the city. This area was important for its inns, few of which now survive although the George and Dragon, much altered, stands at the south-west corner of the open space. Innyards linked the Market Place to a narrow lane at the rear, still called Back of the Inns. One such yard was fashioned into the Royal Arcade in 1899; another, that of the King's Head (made famous by the eighteenth-century diarist Parson Woodforde who habitually stayed there when in Norwich) became Davey Place in 1812.

Despite the substantial changes wrought by the Reformation in the sixteenth century, the dramatic growth in the wealth of the community in the seventeenth century, and the increasingly diverse economy and enhanced fabric of the eighteenth century, Norwich by the 1780s was still an essentially late medieval settlement in appearance. It was densely occupied but almost the entire population was housed within the walls. The situation is well illustrated by the first detailed and accurate map of the city, that of Hochstetter published in 1789. The date is appropriate; the map depicts the medieval and post-medieval city, an *ancien regime* Norwich, at its zenith. Changes in the 1790s heralded the modern world.

8

THE FINE CITY

The antiquity of Norwich was not popular in the late eighteenth century. The greater citizens, worried about the decline in the commercial importance of the city, were anxious to lift some of the burden of inherited medievalism. Agitation was addressed particularly against the city defences with growing calls for their removal. The walls and gates were, in the view of the Norwich Directory of 1783, 'a nuisance, that smells rank in the nose of modern improvement'. Moreover, it was alleged that the existence of the defences inhibited the free movement of air, contributing to unhealthiness in the city. The propaganda was successful and all the city gates were removed between about 1790 and 1810.

The effect, of course, was more symbolic than practical although the removal of the gates certainly reduced obstruction to traffic. The greatest physical effect was upon the surviving walls themselves which ceased to be maintained. In places these too were demolished; parts of the stretch at Bull Close Road were toppled inwards to form a platform for house building. Other stretches fell, as happened at Ber Street in 1807. Elsewhere buildings were erected against the wall, either on the interior next to the intramural lanes such as St Martin-at-Oak Wall Lane or on the exterior as at Magpie Road. Other elements were reused; the remains of a cinder oven survive in the western Boom Tower at Carrow.

SUBURBS AND HOUSING

Development next to the walls obscured the distinctive character of the city and blurred its separation from the countryside. This was exacerbated by the growth of suburbs although these continued to be a slow innovation. Expansion came earliest in the west, with development north of the Newmarket Road outside the City Wall at Crooks Place and Union Place by about 1815. This area, South Heigham or the 'New City', was described as having 'handsome rows of houses' in 1846 although conditions were still poor even for the grander type of house such as those on The Crescent. Here cesspools stood at the backs of houses while buildings in Union Place did not have running water or underground drains.

85 Houses in The Crescent (Brian Ayers)

Very grand planned expansion took place south of the Newmarket Road slightly later in the century by the gradual development of the Town Close estate. The estate had been granted to the mayor, aldermen and citizens by the cathedral priory in 1524 and consisted of a triangular area of land of 111 acres (45ha), bounded by the Ipswich, Newmarket and Eaton Roads. Used for grazing, it was entered by a five-barred gate, which is depicted on Cleer's map of the city in 1696, although by 1750 part of the area was occupied by Town Close House (now a school). A fashionable suburb was created from 1840 onwards, the City maintaining standards by insisting on high-quality workmanship and materials: 'sound Baltic fir, English oak and hard burnt bricks' were all specified while service roads and sewerage systems were also required.

Houses of the growing middle class were also established to the north of the city. Eleven buildings had been erected on St Clement's Hill between 1824 and 1828. These were handsome structures of brick and slate with appropriate supplements; seven of them were furnished with stables. Similarly, about 1830, villas such as The Lawns were built to the east along Thorpe Road while eighteenth-century Georgian development on Bracondale to the south was augmented by large houses such as The Grove.

Elsewhere, the problems of mass housing for an increasing population (it had reached 68,000 by the time of the first census in 1851) were largely contained within the historic core. While expansion in traditional suburbs such as Heigham took place, much early nineteenth-century housing was provided in the centre. It took two forms: consolidation and extension to existing structures; or planned expansion on areas of open space.

The former, a continuation of a tradition extending back to the sixteenth and seventeenth centuries, led to the full development of the typical Norwich 'court'. Large buildings were subdivided and extended with separate households clustering around a central courtyard. In many areas this led rapidly to insanitary slum conditions. Parts of the city became notorious for the abject poverty of the inhabitants and disease was rife. A cholera epidemic in 1850 led to a government report which established that few houses had a water supply and those that did drew water straight from the river; cesspools were in common use and nightsoil was kept in heaps for sale.

The planned developments were obviously better. An early example was Sussex Street, laid out in 1821-4 across part of the Gildencroft between Oak Street and St Augustine's Street. Here the houses on the north side form a large terrace of red brick with decorated doorways while, on the south side, there is a terrace of brick two-storey cottages.

Development in the second half of the nineteenth century was predominantly outside the City Wall, although terraces were constructed within the historic core

86 Sussex Street, intramural development of the 1820s (Brian Ayers)

in places such as Esdelle Street off St Augustine's Street or Synagogue Street off Mountergate and a rather grand terrace was built at the southern end of Surrey Street as late as 1881. Much extramural building took place to the west, off the Dereham, Earlham and Unthank Roads. Terraces to the north were not started until the end of the century.

These terraced houses were of brick, often with the facade being of more fashionable, and more expensive, white brick with red brick at the rear. Roofs were often covered in slate, reflecting the greater availability of materials in the railway age, but traditional pantiles were still used for outhouses and, by the end of the century, were again used on the main house. Sash windows were set in front elevations but, again, traditional casements were frequently retained at the back.

Very many examples of the late nineteenth- and early twentieth-century terraces survive although modernisation of windows and doors continues to remove many details. The design of the houses evolved as they were built; early backs had simple lean-to two-storey extensions while later extensions were gabled. In the early nineteenth century houses were often built two rooms deep with stairs in the rear room. By 1900 a very common plan was for the stairs to rise across the house between front and back rooms. In both cases the buildings lacked a hall although halled examples were also built.

The expansion of the city can obviously be charted in documentation (many of the plans for terraces survive in the city archives as they had to be deposited for scrutiny by city officials for adequate drainage and other facilities) and in the houses themselves. The disposition of many of the streets and houses, however, owed much to the earlier rural topography and this can thus be observed. The triangular nature of the Town Close estate has already been noted, its apex once marked by a gate; similarly, to the north between the Sprowston Road and Magdalen Road, triangular development south of Denmark Road (after the Denmark Farm) is marked at its apex by a large building called Point House. Streets between the Unthank and Newmarket Roads appear to reflect earlier hedgelines between fields. Land ownership, such as that of the Unthank family, also influenced the pattern of development.

INDUSTRY

Housing in the nineteenth and early twentieth centuries therefore changed much of the appearance of the city. Within the historic core, the appearance was also changed by the growth of those industries which provided employment for the expanding population. In many cases traditional activities were maintained. The textile trade continued to be of great importance to the city although it had lost its early eighteenth-century pre-eminence. This was never regained despite

87 St James's Yarn Mill
(Brian Ayers)

valiant attempts to recapture the initiative, most eloquently expressed by the 1836 St James Mill of the Norwich Yarn Company which has been called 'the most noble of all English Industrial Revolution mills' (not an accolade one would expect in Norfolk). The mill was not a success, textile manufacture in 1869 employing only 300 looms, three-fifths of the capacity of the building. The mill still stands, together with its engine house, on the north bank of the river Wensum.

Specialist manufacture of textiles continued throughout the nineteenth century, Norwich being important for the production of silks, crapes and even horse-hair weaving. A crape manufacturer, one John Sultzer, set up a business north of Botolph Street about 1820 next to his house. It is indicative of the amount of open space still available within the walls that he reputedly had a deer park attached to the house as late as 1850!

Leather industries in the nineteenth century were more successful than the textile trades, however, particularly those manufacturing boots and shoes. Shoemakers had long been a distinctive trade within the city and, by the early nineteenth century, companies of some size were coming into existence. One such was that of James Smith which, after 1816, started to mechanise production in St

Peter Mancroft parish (and eventually became the Startrite company). Another was the Norvic company which constructed a purpose-built shoe factory on Colegate in 1856 and again in 1900 (this survives, converted to office use). Over 7000 people were employed in the boot and shoe industry of Norwich by 1901 although not all of these were tied to the large firms; there were still more than 40 'garret masters' active in 1910, producing footwear in traditional small, local workshops.

Food and drink were other Norwich trades which blossomed as major concerns in the nineteenth century. Breweries were common (17 were recorded in 1854) with those such as Steward and Patteson or Bullard of great importance. Bullards built a large brewery on Coslany Street in 1868 with water supplied from an artesian well within the structure; this is now the only major brewery building to survive although it is converted to housing. The roof is supported by cast iron columns, decorated with the anchor motif of the brewery which can also be seen on the surviving base of the adjacent great chimney stack. Part of a light railway line for moving goods within the brewery yard was uncovered in 2007. The offices of Steward and Patteson's brewery also survive, immediately outside the City Wall on Barrack Street, but the rest of the complex was demolished in the 1960s. Brewing continued at Morgan's Brewery on King Street (where massive expansion in 1970 destroyed the site of the Augustinian friary) but ceased in the early 1980s. The Norwich tradition of brewing, including a famous 'Norwich Nog' in the eighteenth century, ceased with it although, since 1981, there has been a revival of brewing by Woodforde's, now based at Woodbastwick outside the city.

A mustard works was established at Carrow by the Colman family, occupying the site of Carrow Priory outside the City Wall. A house was built adjacent to King Street in the 1850s (now in use as offices) with a spectacular conservatory. The earliest factory buildings to survive date from about 1857; they were positioned next to the river so that the works could benefit from water as well as rail transport. Colmans, re-structured into separate companies, still exists as a brand although mustard is no longer produced in Norwich.

Upstream of Colmans, within the City Wall, stands Reads Mill or the Albion Mills (recently converted to housing). These date from the 1830s when they were built as yarn mills but were converted to flour mills in 1932. They supplemented earlier flour mills on Westwick Street, also built in the nineteenth century. Both were located on the river, enabling the use of water transport. Characteristic outshoots for hoists survive on Reads Mill where sacks could be loaded on and off river wherries. The Westwick Mills were destroyed by enemy action in 1942 and Reads Mill ceased production in the spring of 1993.

The structural and mechanical engineering firm of Boulton and Paul was another nineteenth-century company which had great impact upon the topography and

88 Survey drawing of industrial buildings on Fishergate (B. Funnell/Norfolk Industrial Archaeology Society)

89 Light railway line uncovered in yard of former Bullard's Anchor brewery in 2007 (Brian Ayers)

economy of the city. The firm was important for the production of wire netting (the world's earliest netting machine is now in the Bridewell Museum) as well as sectional buildings such as conservatories and, in later years, aircraft frames (including that of the R101 airship). A factory was originally established off Rose Lane in 1865. This grew to occupy most of the block between Mountergate, King Street and Rose Lane by 1898. Demolition of properties in 1899 revealed timbers of a splendid medieval building which were re-used in the company's offices; this building survives on Rose Lane as the Tudor Hall with, to the rear, a prefabricated Boulton and Paul building.

A further engineering company was that of Barnard Bishop Barnard which had established a large iron foundry north of the river in central Norwich about 1855. Among the products of this firm is the cast iron bridge of 1882 linking Barn Road to St Crispin's Road and which still carries the modern Inner Ring Road. Bridges of iron were a feature of Norwich, the Duke's Palace bridge of 1822 (demolished in 1974 but one span now reused within the Castle Mall development) and Foundry Bridge of the 1870s being other examples. The second oldest surviving river bridge in the city is Sir John Soane's bridge on St George's Street; this has a stone arch and dates from 1783 but it also has a cast iron railing which is probably later.

The impact of nineteenth-century industry upon the topography of the walled city is clear from the earliest detailed Ordnance Survey undertaken in 1883 and published in 1885. The number of large-scale institutions, particularly along the river, is striking. To the organisations mentioned above can be added malt houses on Oak Street, a crape manufactory off Westwick Street, timberyards off Colegate, the gasworks north of Bishopgate, further gasworks east of the river at Gas Hill, a major distillery and vinegar works immediately south of the Cathedral Close, brickworks opposite the Close to the east and, finally, timber yards and an ironworks on King Street. Away from the river, Caley's mineral water works behind St Stephen's Street would be redeveloped in 1890 to serve its expanding chocolate business. The new factory had two artesian wells, 400ft (123m) and 500ft (154m) deep. The factory was bombed in 1942, rebuilt after the Second World War and then demolished in 2002 for the new Chapelfield retail and housing development.

URBAN DEVELOPMENT

The large industrial complexes located within and adjacent to the historic core had a profound effect upon the traditional topography of the city. Some, such as Colman's, were built on marginal sites but the acquisition of an area such as the Rose Lane works of Boulton and Paul could only be established by the amalgamation and demolition of many adjacent properties.

In these circumstances it is surprising that streets were not lost as well as many tenement and other boundaries. One street which was closed was that of World's End Lane which ran east of St Martin-at-Palace Plain. The gasworks was constructed north of this street in the 1850s (destroying the medieval town house of Sir Thomas Erpingham) but expansion in 1888 removed the lane. The Colman family succeeded in diverting King Street slightly to the west, thus ensuring that their house would have a carriage drive sheltered from the street. As late as 1920 the Colman company managed to get the line of Carrow Road diverted with the construction of a new swing bridge just inside the Boom Towers. This enabled demolition of the original Carrow Bridge which had carried the road through the middle of the factory site.

New streets were created within the historic centre. The construction of Davey Place in 1813 has been mentioned above. Exchange Street was built north of the Market Place by 1828. Later in the century, the most notable new thoroughfare was made, that of Prince of Wales Road. This was planned as a great sweeping curve from the centre of the city to Thorpe Railway Station. It was laid out in 1864 and development at the city end was splendid but investment ran out at the lower end of the street and the design was never completed. It is probable that substantial elements of the Franciscan friary were uncovered during its construction; an un-provenanced plan purporting to show the church may date from this time.

South of the city a road was created up Carrow Hill, a scheme initiated as poor relief. A similar scheme led to the construction of Gurney Road from Barrack Street to the Salhouse Road through Mousehold Heath. The remnants of this heath, which in the sixteenth century had extended some nine miles (15km) eastward as far as Ranworth, amounted to 184 acres (74ha) by 1883 when they were granted by the Dean and Chapter to the citizens of Norwich as a recreational resource.

Communications by road and water were, of course, supplemented by railways in the mid-nineteenth century. The first railway was constructed between Norwich and Yarmouth in 1845, a terminus being provided at Thorpe Railway Station, immediately east of the river Wensum. This station was replaced by the existing station in 1886 but engine sheds of the 1840s survived until the 1990s, the earliest such buildings in East Anglia (they were demolished, ahead of possible listing, prior to redevelopment of the extensive area of marshalling yards). Extension of the railway network led to the creation of two further stations, both also on the edge of the historic core. The City Station was built at Barn Road in 1882; bombed in 1942 it lingered until final demolition in 1960. The Victoria Station of 1849 was situated on Queen's Road. It was demolished and became a coal yard although it is now commemorated in fanciful fake 'ironwork' on the supermarket which stands on the site.

The physical legacy of nineteenth- and early twentieth-century industrial Norwich is still strong but much has been destroyed. Extraordinary buildings such as the St James Mill do survive as do structures like the showrooms of Holmes & Sons on Cattle Market Street (engineers who were taken over by Panks in 1902), with a splendid cast iron and glass front of the 1860s. Losses, however, while including such important complexes as those of Boulton and Paul on Rose Lane (except the Tudor Hall) and the Barnard Bishop Barnard site, also embrace buildings of less well-known companies. A 1903 cloth factory of the company Messrs Roberts on Botolph Street was demolished in 1967. Built by A.F. Scott, this building has been described as of European importance in the 1997 edition of Pevsner's 'The Buildings of England'. The 1962 edition not only illustrated the building but stated that 'there was little in England or indeed in Europe quite so functional and unfussy' and drew excited comparison with the Glasgow School of Art.

Losses continue; an unlisted maltings, the last in the city, was demolished recently as part of development around the Norwich City football stadium.

PUBLIC BUILDINGS

The nineteenth century was also a period when great public buildings were constructed. One of the earliest was the Shirehall of William Wilkins which was built in 1822-3, shortly before the construction of his main entrance and perimeter wall to the gaol (now the Castle Museum) of about 1825. The Shirehall was extended in 1906, prompting archaeological observation by E.J. Tench who published a section of the castle mound where the building cut into early deposits. The Norfolk and Norwich Subscription Library was constructed in 1835; it still stands but its books have been transferred to the University of East Anglia and the Norwich School. A new fish market was built in 1860; the Guildhall and St Andrew's Hall were both restored and embellished in the 1860s; a Corn Exchange was erected in 1863 (now lamentably demolished); the Agricultural Hall dates from 1882 (currently studios and offices of Anglia Television); and the Technical Institute (now Norwich University College of Art) was built in 1899.

Outside the City Walls, St Andrew's Hospital was built in 1811-14 as a mental institution. Until closure and conversion to housing in the 1990s, it was the oldest such functioning institution in the country. At the Great Hospital, provision for old age included the installation of cubicles for men and women in the western and eastern parts of the medieval building by 1839 at the latest. These remained in use into the 1980s.

Alterations and additions were also made to the Norfolk and Norwich Hospital, notably in 1879-84 when Edward Boardman created a 'Nightingale' hospital following the principles of care laid down by Florence Nightingale. The hospital

90 The Shirehall by William Wilkins, 1822 (Brian Ayers)

closed in 2001 and was largely demolished, the gable ends of the nightingale wings being retained and earlier eighteenth-century buildings converted to new use.

Military building had started in 1791 with the Cavalry Barracks on Barrack Street. These occupied the site of The Lathes, a grange of the medieval cathedral priory subsequently called Blennerhasset House. The barracks in turn were demolished in the early 1970s as was the Drill Hall of 1866 on Chapelfield Road together with a tower of the medieval City Wall which had been incorporated into it. The Britannia Barracks of the Norfolk and Norwich Regiment survive, however, on Britannia Road. These date from 1885-7 and retain details such as an integrated sentry box.

Public investment gradually extended to the provision of public services. Street paving initiatives, such as covering Gentleman's Walk in York stone in 1863, were followed by sewage and slum clearance schemes. The first sewers were laid in 1869 and it was the provision of other sewers in 1896 between Elm Hill and Colegate, across the river Wensum, which led to one of the most startling archaeological observations of the nineteenth century, that of a pre-Conquest causeway structure.

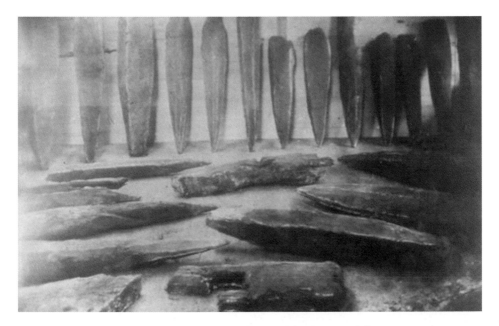

91 Causeway bridge piles recovered in 1896 from Fye Bridge (Norfolk Museums & Archaeology Service)

ANTIQUARIAN STUDY

This causeway was seen and reported by the Reverend William Hudson, one of the greatest of Norwich antiquaries (*colour plate 30*). He lived at a time when others were also noting the material history of the city, often as a result of observation of a rapidly changing environment. While slum clearance, which started as early as 1877, did not necessarily attract attention (the antiquarian importance of some of the buildings was probably not appreciated), Hudson, with the likes of Beecheno and Rye, pursued disparate interests and enthusiasms, laying a basis for much modern archaeological work.

Rye and Beecheno were pioneers of architectural conservation. Rye might have been scathing about 'the Society for the Prevention of Cruelty to Ancient Buildings' but he also took an active role in preserving ancient structures in the city, purchasing the early twelfth-century Lazar House to save it from demolition. Beecheno too was active in such matters, writing in strong terms to the City Council in 1885 to protest at a breach which had been made for a new doorway in the north, flint-knapped and squared, wall of the Bridewell.

The nineteenth-century city was therefore one which, while being modernised, also housed those who cared about its past. Such care was, of course, limited by commercial pressures which remained of paramount importance. George Borrow could write in lyrical terms about the city in 1851 as:

92 Drawing by John Sell Cotman of Norwich Castle Bridge under repair in the late 1820s (Norfolk Museums & Archaeology Service)

93 Excavations in Norwich Castle keep in 1889 (Norfolk Museums & Archaeology Service)

A fine old city, truly, is that, view it from whatever side you will ... perhaps the
most curious specimen at present extant of the genuine old English town. Yes,
there it spreads ... with its venerable houses, its numerous gardens, its thrice twelve
churches ... a grey old castle ... and yonder, rising three hundred feet above the soil
... behold that old Norman master-work, that cloud-encircled cathedral spire ...

But the 1850s was also the decade which saw the establishment of the gasworks
immediately north of the cathedral precinct (it was removed in 1970).

PUBLIC UTILITIES AND CHURCHES

Gas provision was not new in the 1850s; gas pipes were first laid in 1820 and
soon afterwards a 'gasolier' had been erected on the Market Place with four gas
lamps. Water supply began to improve after a new water works with a filtration
system was established at New Mills in mid-century. The building was adapted
as a compression house in 1897 to pump sewage. Its compressed air machinery
survives. Municipal cemeteries were provided, firstly at Rosary Road about
1819, the earliest in the country, and then off Earlham Road in 1865. Both retain
tombs and tombstones of ornate Victorian design. Late in the century schools
were built, such as the Angel Road Boys School of 1895.

Public conveniences, male only at first, were built on Tombland in 1878. Others
followed at sites such as the forecourt of St Andrew's Hall. A 'Clochemelle' style
urinal was established by the early twentieth century in the middle of the north
end of Tombland; it was removed in 1919 to be replaced by a pedestal bust
of Edith Cavell (itself now moved to a less exposed location adjacent to the
cathedral precinct wall). Of greatest interest is a urinal of patterned concrete
with a glazed roof on Station Road (now St Crispin's Road). Earlier examples
are known from Paris but this structure is probably one of the earliest surviving
concrete urinals in the world and is now listed.

Increasing care of the physical wellbeing of the population was matched by
provision for the spirit. The ancient city remained well-endowed with churches
(too well-endowed; the church of St Peter Southgate was allowed to fall into
ruins in 1887, the first loss of a medieval church since the sixteenth century;
a fragment of the tower arch survives) but new churches were needed in the
growing suburbs. The earliest was that of Christ Church, New Catton, built in
1841-2. It was followed by St Mark, Hall Road (1844), St Matthew, Rosary
Road (1851), Holy Trinity, Essex Street (1860-1), St Philip, Heigham Road
(1871), Christ Church, Church Avenue (1874) and St Thomas, Earlham Road
(1886). This last was badly damaged in the Second World War and rebuilt while
St Philip was demolished in the 1970s; the others survive.

Left: 94 Public urinal, Station Road (Brian Ayers)

Below: 95 St John the Baptist, Earlham Road (Norwich HEART)

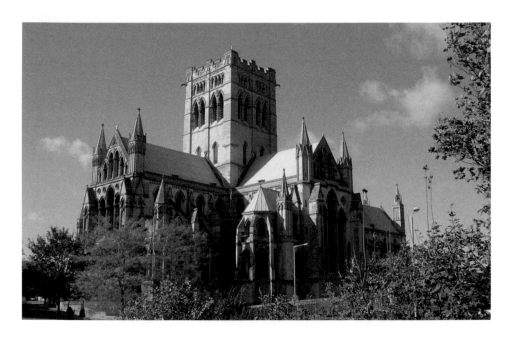

The greatest church to be built in the nineteenth century, however, was that of St John the Baptist, Earlham Road. This was paid for by the Duke of Norfolk and constructed, on the site of the City Gaol of 1827, to designs of George Gilbert Scott Jr as a church for the Roman Catholic community. Scott was certified insane in 1884 and the building was completed by his brother John Oldrid Scott. It is an enormous building in Early English revival style with a length of 275 ft (85m). Not always loved (it has been described as 'severe, chaste and forbidding') it is also seen as 'proof of Victorian generosity and optimism'. Since 1976, it has been designated as the cathedral church of the Roman Catholic diocese of East Anglia.

Chapels were also built, some of them exceptionally large. The Congregational Church on Princes Street is a good example, a yellow brick building of 1869 in the classical style. This remains in use as does the Friends Meeting House of 1826 on Upper Goat Lane and the Methodist Chapel on Chapelfield Road. Others also survive, often adapted for re-use such as the former Catholic chapel of 1827 on Willow Lane. Others still have been demolished, losses including the 1810 Methodist church on Calvert Street, the 1811 Baptist chapel on Colegate or the Wesleyan chapel of 1858 in Ber Street.

COMMERCIAL BUILDINGS

Commercial development in the late nineteenth century continued to provide Norwich with some of its finest Victorian buildings. The old Post Office at the top of Prince of Wales Road, originally built as a bank in 1886, was converted to form offices for Anglia Television in 1979/80 and has recently been converted again as apartments. A dramatic building faced in limestone with a portico of Ionic columns, it stands opposite the Royal Hotel, built by Edward Boardman in 1896-7 with turrets and ornate decorated brickwork. Another local architect, George Skipper, created the Royal Arcade in 1899 as a tremendous Arts and Crafts structure.

Skipper's work continued into the twentieth century when he was commissioned to design the headquarters building of 1903-4 for Norwich Union. This sumptuous structure, with its great marble hall (*colour plate 31*), replaced Surrey House which had been built about 1540. He also designed the ornate Jarrolds shop of 1903-5 and Telephone House in St Giles Street in 1906, a flamboyant Edwardian baroque building.

Norwich, on the eve of the First World War, was thus a typical provincial city with a diverse economic base. It still suffered from overcrowding and slum conditions in the city centre but these began to be addressed as soon as the war was over. A council estate at Mile Cross, the first such in the country, was built between 1918-23 as a civic initiative. From 1924 central government funds were

96 Norwich Union
headquarters, Surrey Street
(Norwich HEART)

available for slum clearance and rehousing. Expansion of the city gathered pace,
particularly to the north, west and east.

BETWEEN THE WARS

The growth of new estates took over farmland, the old farmhouses and cottages
frequently surviving among the interwar developments. Examples exist on
Wroxham Road and Woodcock Road. City centre development continued as
well, the greatest development of all being that of the City Hall which was
completed in1938. This majestic brick building, 'the foremost English public
building of between the wars', dominates a refurbished market place and
replaced late nineteenth-century municipal buildings and the medieval Guildhall
(the latter being retained).

Construction of the City Hall entailed demolition of considerable numbers
of earlier buildings as did the continuing programme of slum clearance. While
the social benefits were clearly great, the archaeological and architectural loss
was also significant. The absence of any detailed examination of such structures
before clearance meant that the demolition of hundreds of individual properties

resulted in the loss not only of fine buildings but also of enormous quantities of information on the social and economic development of the city.

There were those who recognised that the price being paid for modernising the city was too high. In 1923 the Norwich Society, the first civic society in the country, was formed with aims 'to stimulate historic interest in the City as a civic pride amongst its citizens; to pursue all things of beauty; all buildings and objects of antiquarian and architectural worth; to exercise vigilant opposition to all acts of vandalism and generally to work for a fairer city'. Objectors in the 1930s successfully prevented the destruction of St Stephen's Street, notably the Boar's Head, a celebrated tavern, while Elm Hill, now the city's most famous street, was saved from redevelopment as an industrial estate by the casting vote of the mayor.

THE SECOND WORLD WAR

Destruction was accelerated, however, by the Second World War. The city was subjected to 'Baedeker' raids in April 1942 which left much of the south-western part of the historic core in ruins. By the end of the war, bombing had destroyed the medieval churches of St Benedict, St Michael-at-Thorn, St Paul and St Julian (the last rebuilt post-war) as well as the remains of St Bartholomew and the suburban medieval church of St Bartholomew, Heigham.

The south transept of the cathedral church was hit by incendiaries, St Stephen's Street was devastated (including, ironically, the Boar's Head Inn), the Midland and Great Northern City Station was badly damaged and late medieval and post-medieval houses were wrecked across the city. Even today an unexploded bomb lies buried close to the north transept of the cathedral; it fell into a well and efforts to dig it out were unavailing.

The end of the war led to reconstruction and, as in many other British cities, to a paradoxical extension of the attack upon the historic environment, an attack that continued with little official regard for recording or conservation until the 1970s. Losses include the whole of St Stephen's Street, a long stretch of the city wall up Grape's Hill (including two towers and, possibly, the buried remains of St Giles Gate), Stump Cross and much of Botolph Street, the site of the Augustinian friary, the site (and probably some buildings) of the Cloth Seld (the medieval cloth hall), the galleried White Swan Inn together with its vaulted undercrofts, and the New Star Inn on Quayside. This last, demolished in 1963, was condemned by one councillor, in a statement which may be apocryphal but which has the ring of truth, as it was known to have been used as a brothel at some time in the past and 'we don't want buildings like that in the city, do we?'.

To balance these losses, the city has been enhanced by a number of developments. Within the historic core bold buildings have been erected for the Central Library

97 The fifteenth-century New Star Inn on Quayside prior to demolition (George Plunkett)

98 Refectory building at Norwich Cathedral (Brian Ayers)

(David Percival1962; destroyed by fire in 1994), Eastern Counties Newspapers (Yates Cook & Derbyshire1970), Anglia Television (Feilden & Mawson1980), the Bank of Scotland (Lambert Scott & Innes1988) and the Castle Mall shopping centre (Lambert Scott & Innes1993). In 2001, the destroyed library was replaced by a landmark Millennium building designed by Michael Hopkins Partnership and a passenger lift has been inserted in the castle mound (Purcell Miller Tritton 2001). Hopkins also designed the refectory building at the cathedral (above the remains of the medieval refectory) and work is currently proceeding on a further Hopkins design for a new hostry building for the cathedral.

Within the area of the greater city notable structures have been built at the University of East Anglia (by Denys Lasdun) together with the Sainsbury Centre and Crescent Wing (by Norman Foster) and the Climatic Research Unit and New Residences (by Rick Mather). At Bowthorpe, a group of three linked villages was established in the 1970s and early 1980s as an initiative of the City Council.

The growth of housing, particularly in the city centre, has been considerable in recent years. An early experiment was constructed at Friars Quay in 1974 by Feilden and Mawson. Some 40 houses replaced a timber yard and are distinguished by steeply pitched roofs and a massing which is much admired. Its central riverside location is not the only one to be so exploited. Conversion of Bullards Brewery to housing took place in the 1980s, there has been considerable residential development off Oak Street in the 1990s, modern apartments have recently been constructed on Fishergate and off Duke Street (*colour plate 32*), and new housing stands on King Street and Quayside.

One of the more visible legacies of the post-war period in the historic core, however, is not so much new building, which frequently enhances the city, but the way in which the ancient topography was distorted in the years up to about 1975. Streets, for example, were widened where possible. This has resulted in continuing absurdities, such as Pottergate where a great and narrow medieval street is interrupted at one point by a modern suite of shops set back from the frontage. The shops themselves would probably escape much notice if aligned with everything else; as it is attention is drawn to them, not necessarily favourably.

The lesson to be drawn from the modern development of the city is that the continued and necessary transformation of Norwich works best in concert with the inherited environment rather than against it. Appreciating this lesson has required a new image of the city. 'Historic Norwich' as a concept has needed to embrace the entire city, not just the obviously antique. At the same time, the economic importance of the inherited environment has needed recognition. The two are now encapsulated in a new agency, Norwich Heart (Heritage Economic & Regeneration Trust) which has a strategic mission to 'plan, regenerate, manage and promote Norwich's heritage resources and act as a best practice case study nationally and internationally for developing heritage as a vehicle for social and economic regeneration'. This brave approach is the legacy of a gradually increasing awareness of the value of the historic environment, a value generated in large part by detailed study of the city, not least the archaeological study of buried deposits as well as standing buildings.

ARCHAEOLOGY SINCE 1945

Post-war archaeological work began in 1946 with excavations conducted by the late Martyn Jope on behalf of the Norfolk and Norwich Archaeological Society. Further work was undertaken in the 1950s and 1960s by John Hurst, Rainbird Clarke and Barbara Green but it was only in 1971 that an archaeological unit was established, the Norwich Survey, which allowed a co-ordinated approach involving the study of buildings, documents and archaeology.

Work since 1979, largely by the Norfolk Archaeological Unit, has sought to continue this approach, employing new techniques as they are developed. Archaeological activity in the city is now much more common, in itself forming part of the history of Norwich. It would be churlish, also, to ignore the many other contributions to a greater understanding of the development of the city and its

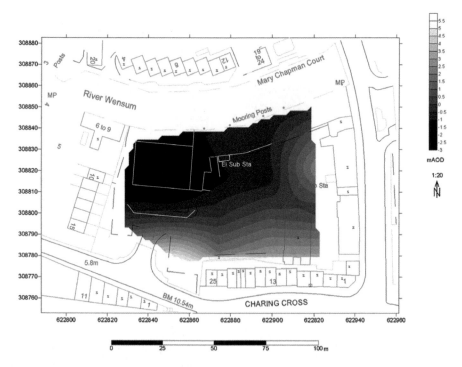

99 Modern archaeological approaches: results of 'window'-sampling at Duke Street showing infilling next to the river (NAU Archaeology)

society which have taken place in the modern period. Studies as disparate as those of church bells and ledger slabs, Norwich as a centre of eighteenth-century dissent or even the contribution of Norwich to the history of the telephone exchange have been undertaken, all contributing to knowledge of the growth of the city.

It is therefore necessary, at the end of a work devoted to an appraisal of the development of a great provincial city, to summarise the results of archaeological work and interpretation over the last 50 years.

There is now a much clearer understanding of the origins of the city although, for the period prior to the eleventh century, the view is still one of through a glass, darkly. The development of hinterland studies is nevertheless enabling the rural context for the early growth of the city to be better understood, methodological approaches continue to develop (not least with regard to

100 Zipfel House of 2005 with City Wall at site of Magdalen Gate

enhanced understanding of the palaeogeography of the urban landscape) and excavation is slowly increasing the quantity of information available within Norwich. Considerable light is being shed on the Anglo-Scandinavian and Saxo-Norman periods when Norwich rapidly gained pre-eminence amongst the towns of East Anglia. Evidence for the society, economy and commerce of the settlement continues to be unearthed, enabling greater definition of the nature and importance of the Conquest period town.

For the medieval period, the integrated approach of documents, buildings and excavation is continuing to provide a much more detailed understanding of the social structure of the city and of the institutions and buildings which supported it. Study of the urban population is being enhanced by a greater awareness of economic conditions as well as by detailed demographic analysis, particularly of skeletal groups.

This integrated approach is also of exceptional use for the post-medieval period although here work has not been as intensive as that for earlier centuries. Nevertheless, understanding of the urban fabric, local industry and social conditions has increased dramatically in the last 20 years. This is especially the case with appreciation of nineteenth- and twentieth-century development. It is now becoming much more common for thorough appraisal of industrial structures to be undertaken, for instance, prior to finalisation of proposals for re-use.

Overall, archaeological work continues to yield much information about the pre-urban and urban environment and changes to that environment wrought by people through time. It has defined areas of occupation, isolated hidden aspects of the topography and identified processes of change. It is providing information on the daily concerns of the population of Norwich in the past – food, shelter and employment. It is exploring the church and the great urban institutions, lay as well as ecclesiastic. It is helping to increase understanding of trade, commercial and cultural contacts across northern Europe.

Future archaeological work in the city will inevitably be dictated, at least in part, by development pressure. It can, nevertheless, be driven by research goals. A Research Framework for East Anglia has now been produced with a chapter devoted to urban priorities. These highlight the importance of archaeology to the study of demography, social organisation, the economy, culture and religion. Within a Norwich context, work can also seek to explain the success of the city in its region and its significance nationally.

Perhaps the greatest continuing contribution of archaeology to Norwich, however, is that it encourages a perception of the city as a single entity, one changing continuously but with a present integrated with the past. This recognition allows future planning to be undertaken as part of the historic environment. Archaeology is the study of change. The physical shape of the city is the product of such change in the past; archaeological research is the beneficiary of such change in the present; its gift is an understanding of the processes of change to the future.

CHRONOLOGICAL SUMMARY

SUMMARY TABLE OF EVENTS

*c.*720	Establishment of small villages on both banks of river Wensum
*c.*850	probable dominance of one settlement – *Northwic*
*c.*870-917	Probable Danish occupation; construction of defensive earthwork on north bank
917	Conquest of East Anglia by Edward the Elder Probable use of Norwich as administrative centre
924-939	Reign of Aethelstan. Coins minted in Norwich
*c.*980	First documentary reference to Norwich (in *Liber Eliensis*)
1004	Norwich sacked by the Danes
1066	Entry in Domesday Book (1086) suggests Norwich had at least 25 churches as well as 1320 burgesses
1068-1075	Establishment of castle and 'French Borough'
1075	Siege of Norwich Castle
1086	Domesday Book entry; number of burgesses fallen to 650
1094	Establishment of the cathedral
*c.*1120	Expansion south along King Street
*c.*1140	Expansion north-east of the river
1174	Sack of Norwich by Flemings
1216	Castle falls to Louis, Dauphin of France
1226	Establishment of first friary (Franciscans)
1266	The 'Disinherited' raid Norwich
*c.*1280-1340	Construction of the city wall
1349	Black Death
1398/9	Cow Tower built
1404	Charter creates offices of mayor and aldermen
1410	Guildhall under construction
1430	City water mills built
Fifteenth century	Considerable rebuilding of churches
1507	Disastrous fires
1536-1539	Dissolution of the Monasteries
1549	City besieged during Kett's Rebellion
1565 onward	Settling of 'Strangers' in Norwich
1578	Visit of Elizabeth I
1648	Civil War riot
*c.*1660-*c.*1730	'Second City' of England in terms of wealth
1790-1810	Demolition of the city gates
Nineteenth century	Development of printing, leather, food industries
1930s	Slum clearance
1942	'Baedeker' air raids
1945	City of Norwich Plan
1948	First post-war archaeological excavation
1950s/1960s	Excavations by Norfolk Research Committee
1971-1978	Excavations by the Norwich Survey
1979-present	Excavations by the Norfolk Archaeological Unit (now NAU Archaeology)

FURTHER READING

Norwich's lack of a thorough and up-to-date history of the city has been addressed recently by the publication of a two-volume work. *Medieval Norwich* and *Norwich since 1560* (London 2004), both edited by Carole Rawcliffe and Richard Wilson. Together these two books contain 32 papers on the city. Good introductions remain that of Barbara Green and Rachel Young, *Norwich: the growth of a city* (Norwich, revised edition 1981) or James Campbell's essay in the *Historic Towns* series: 'Norwich' in M.D. Lobel (ed.), *Historic Towns II* (London 1975). Malcolm Atkin's useful *Norwich: history and guide* was published in 1993 (Stroud) while Frank Meeres produced *A History of Norwich* in 1998 (Chichester) wherein information drawn from post-medieval documentation is of particular interest.

Important books which deal with specific topics but which have a national interest are V.D. Lipman, *The Jews of Medieval Norwich* (London 1967) and N.P. Tanner, *The Church in late Medieval Norwich 1370 – 1532* (Toronto 1984). A survey of *Tudor and Stuart Norwich* was published by John Pound in 1988 (Chichester) and a volume on *Norwich in the Nineteenth Century* was edited by Chris Barringer in 1984 (Norwich).

Notwithstanding the recent two-volume publication, an indispensible survey remains that of Francis Blomefield, originally published in the eighteenth century but most commonly available in the 1806 edition of his *An Essay towards a Topographical History of the County of Norfolk, continued by Parkin*, Vols. III and IV (Norwich) and now also available online (see below). Other early works of great importance for an understanding of the topographical growth of Norwich are those of John Kirkpatrick, especially *The Streets and Lanes of Norwich: a memoir*, edited by W.H. Hudson (Norwich 1889). Hudson himself was a great contributor to the study of Norwich, editing (with J.C. Tingey) a two-volume edition of *The Records of the City of Norwich* (Norwich 1906 and 1910).

There are numerous works on aspects of Norwich although the most influential for the pre-Conquest period remains a journal paper by the late Alan Carter, 'The Anglo-Saxon Origins of Norwich: the problems and approaches' (*Anglo-Saxon England 7*, 1978, 175 - 204) – although outdated, it is full of ideas and contains a wealth of useful references. A successor paper by the present writer entitled 'The Growth of an Urban Landscape: Recent Research in Early Medieval Norwich' will be published soon. The Domesday Book entry for Norwich is available in both transcription and translation: P. Brown (ed.), *Domesday Book: Norfolk* (Chichester 1984) and the volume concerning place-names within the walls has also been published: K.I Sandred and B. Lindstrom, 'Place-Names of the City of Norwich', *The Place-Names of Norfolk*, Part 1 (English Place-Name Society 1989). The plans of the city have recently been comprehensively re-assessed by Raymond Frostick in *The Printed Plans of Norwich 1558-1840: a carto-bibliography* (2002, privately published by the author but available *via* the internet). This work both updates and supersedes the earlier work by Chubb and Stephen (*Norfolk Maps and Norwich Plans*, Norwich 1928) which has been out-of-print for many years.

A great deal has been written on aspects of the architecture, archaeology, artefacts and documentation of medieval and post-medieval Norwich with a number of works appearing in recent years. Evidence for housing in the twelfth and thirteenth centuries has been summarised along with material from elsewhere in England and France, in Dominique Pitte and Brian Ayers, *La Maison Médiévale/The Medieval House*, Rouen 2002) although the most recent summaries of surveys of important Norwich buildings such as Strangers Hall, Suckling Hall and the King of Hearts are unpublished, only having appeared in conference notes for the *Vernacular Architecture Group* (by Robert Smith in 1997). Chris King has produced an exceptionally interesting and useful thesis on the surviving houses of the late medieval and early post-medieval urban élite (University of Reading, unpublished). A major work on the churches of Norwich remains to be written although two recent publications are of particular note: Barbara Crawford on St Clement churches, referencing the two such churches in Norwich, 'The Churches dedicated to St Clement in Medieval England' in *Scripta ecclesiastica* (St Petersburg 2008); and David King's comprehensive work entitled 'The Medieval Stained Glass of St Peter Mancroft Norwich', *Corpus Vitrearum Medii Aevi* vol V (British Academy 2006).

Reports concerning the archaeology of the city are largely available as academic monographs, papers in local or national journals, or as slim, popular publications. Many have been drawn upon for this work, too many to acknowledge individually here. The most common source is *Norfolk Archaeology*, the journal of the Norfolk and Norwich Archaeological Society, which has published papers on the history and archaeology of Norwich since 1846. The seven parts issued between 1972-78 contain interim reports of the work of the Norwich Survey while, since this book was first published in 1994, work on recent survey or excavation in the city has appeared in the volumes for 1996, 1997, 1999, 2001, 2004, 2005 and 2007.

The principal publication route for most excavations undertaken in the city and its vicinity in the last 30 years, however, is the journal series *East Anglian Archaeology* (volumes 13, 15, 17, 26, 28, 37, 58, 68, 91, 92, 96, 100, 112, 116 and 120 to date – see www.eaareports.org.uk for details). Several popular publications have also been issued concerning work by the Norwich Survey (M.W. Atkin and S. Margeson, *Life on a Medieval Street*, Norwich 1985) and the Norfolk Archaeological Unit (B.S. Ayers, *Digging under the Doorstep*, Norwich 1983; B.S. Ayers, *Digging Deeper*, Norwich 1987; and B.S. Ayers, J. Bown and J. Reeve, *Digging Ditches*, Norwich 1992). A special edition of *Current Archaeology* (no. 170 – October 2000), which was devoted to the archaeology of the city, provides a useful update on work in the 1990s.

Individual monuments have been the subject of a number of volumes. The cathedral has naturally received most attention. Two works mentioned in 1994, the publication of John Adey Repton's survey of *c.*1800 (*Norwich Cathedral at the end of the eighteenth century*, Farnborough 1965) and Eric Fernie's book *An Architectural History of Norwich Cathedral* (Oxford 1993), were supplemented by a handsome third volume in 1996 when the ninth centenary of the cathedral was marked by publication of *Norwich Cathedral: church, city and diocese 1096-1996* edited by Ian Atherton, Eric Fernie, Christopher Harper-Bill and Hassell Smith (London 1996). Other works include *Stories in Stone: the medieval roof carvings of Norwich Cathedral* by Martial Rose and Julia Hedgecoe (London, 1997) as well as publications on aspects of a thorough re-survey of the cathedral church and its attendant buildings in the 1990s (plus observations during conservation work) by Roberta Gilchrist (*Journal of the British Archaeological Association* 151, 1999 and *The Archaeological Journal* 158, 2001). Roberta Gilchrist has also produced the most significant and ground-breaking book on the historic environment of Norwich in recent years with her publication *Norwich Cathedral Close: the Evolution of the English Cathedral Landscape* (Woodbridge 2005).

The castle is less-well known although recent assessments of the keep have been published as two papers in the same volume: P. Drury 'Norwich Castle Keep' and P. Dixon & P. Marshall 'Norwich castle and its analogues', both in G. Meirion-Jones *et al* (eds.) *The Seigneurial Residence in Western Europe AD c800 – 1600* (BAR International Series 1088, 2002). The substantial reports on the massive excavations which took place in and around the south bailey in 1989-91 and on the southern defences in 1998 should be published in *East Anglian Archaeology* in 2009. Work continues on the report of the sections through the great mound in 1999-2001. Andy Shelley published the results of survey and excavation of the castle bridge in 1996 ('Norwich Castle Bridge', *Medieval Archaeology* 40) while Sandy Heslop produced a magisterial account of the keep in 1994 (T.A. Heslop, *Norwich Castle Keep*, Norwich).

Carole Rawliffe published her work on the remarkable documentation of St Giles Hospital in *Medicine for the Soul: the life, death and resurrection of an English medieval hospital* (Stroud, 1999). She also produced a detailed work entitled *The Hospitals of Medieval Norwich* (Norwich, 1995). The nunnery at Carrow, and other Norwich institutions, form part of the book *Religious Women in Medieval East Anglia* by Roberta Gilchrist and Marilyn Oliva (Norwich, 1993).

Norwich monuments and archaeology are naturally covered in synthetic works such as *The Normans in Norfolk* (edited by Sue Margeson, Fabienne Seillier and Andrew Rogerson in 1994) and *A Festival of Norfolk Archaeology* (edited by Sue Margeson, Brian Ayers and Stephen Heywood in 1996). Sue Margeson completed the text of her *The Vikings in Norfolk* shortly before her untimely death and it includes a number of Viking artefacts from the city (Norwich, 1997). The proceedings of the biennial *Lübecker Kolloquium zur Stadtarchäologie in Hanseraum* (Lübeck, 1999, 2001, 2003, 2006, 2008 and forthcoming) include respectively summaries by the present writer on the trade, housing, infrastructure, crafts & industries, luxury and defences of medieval and early post-medieval Norwich.

Festschriften contain a number of papers on Norwich such as *East Anglian Studies*, presented to Chris Barringer and edited by Adam Longcroft and Richard Joby in 1995 (Norwich) or *Counties and Communities* presented to Hassell Smith and edited by Carole Rawcliffe, Roger Virgoe and Richard Wilson in 1996 (Norwich). Norwich also provides much data for Bärbel Brodt's 1997 book *Städte ohne Mauern: Stadtentwicklung in East Anglia im 14. Jahrhundert* (Paderborn – but only available in German).

The volume entitled *North-East Norfolk and Norwich* by Nikolaus Pevsner in the Buildings of England series was updated by Bill Wilson in 1997 (Harmondsworth). It provides a comprehensive and valuable guide with a wide range of 'perambulations'.

As before, the best approach to the variety of publications concerning the city is probably through the Norfolk Bibliography. Two volumes of *A Bibliography of Norfolk History* have been published (Norwich 1975, compiled and edited by E. Darroch and B. Taylor; and Norwich 1991 compiled and edited by B. Taylor). Norwich also has an urban archaeological database as part of the Norfolk Historic Environment Record (NHER). This record can be accessed online at www.heritage. norfolk.gov.uk and contains digital copies of recent short reports produced for desk-based assessments, evaluation excavations, watching briefs and surveys.

Online resources are developing rapidly. Recent additions directly relevant to Norwich are the Great Hospital website www.thegreathospital.co.uk, that for Norwich textiles www.norwichtextiles.org.uk and the extraordinary archive of photographs taken from the 1930s onward by George Plunkett in both black-and-white and colour www.georgeplunkett.co.uk. The website for Norwich Heart www.heritagecity.org contains numerous useful links. Perhaps the greatest recent addition, however, has been that of the two Norwich volumes of Blomefield's *Topographical History* which can be accessed at www.british-history.ac.uk/catalogue.aspx?gid=139.

INDEX

Grid references in squared brackets after street-names refer to illustrations on pp.14-15. Churches and religious houses are located on the same pages.